YOUR FUTURE REFLECTION

HOW TO LEAVE
A LEGACY BEYOND MONEY

GUY HATCHER

But Abram said, "Sovereign Lord, what can you give me
since I remain childless and the one who will inherit
my estate is Eliezer of Damascus?"
Genesis 15:2 NIV

Abraham left everything he owned to [his son] Isaac.
But while he was still living, he gave gifts to the sons of
his concubines and sent them away from his son
Isaac to the land of the east.
Genesis 25:5-6 NIV

DEDICATION PAGE

To all the families who have allowed me to participate in your futures: thank you for entrusting me with your time as well as the management of your resources.

To my dear wife, Tamera, and two precious daughters, thank you for providing the reason behind why this book is so important to me, our family, and our future.

Most importantly, I thank my God, who placed this call on my heart and provided me with the truth, promise, ability, and plan to truly have a great impact in the lineage of my family for many years to come.

TABLE OF CONTENTS

INTRODUCTION

YOUR FUTURE REFLECTION:

HOW TO LEAVE A LEGACY BEYOND MONEY

"YOUR BALL IS NEAR the cedar tree about fifteen yards past the two large oak trees sitting side by side to the right of the fairway," Jim explained for the second time. I walked in the direction of the trees in total disgust and frustration—wondering to myself what was so difficult about keeping that little white ball in the middle of the wide, manicured fairway.

Sure enough, as I neared the tree, about fifty yards down the fairway off to the right, sat my second shot. It was exactly where Jim had indicated. Over the years of playing golf together, Jim had demonstrated an uncanny ability to track and locate lost golf balls. But he wasn't only gifted on the golf course. He had a keen ability to see into a difficult situation, identify the root problem, determine a corrective process, and direct others toward success.

I enjoyed the time I spent with Jim, and over months of working together, he grew to be more than just another business client of mine. He became a mentor and trusted friend.

Jim was a remarkable American success story. In the late seventies he completed his Bachelor's of Science degree in engineering and married his sweetheart, Evelyn. At a time when the typical graduate was looking for a safe place to land on a large corporate ladder, Jim itched to strike out on his own and boot-strap a business from the ground up. If you recall the Carter era, you'll remember it as a time of high inflation, soaring interest rates, and economic volatility. All of this combined to make launching a start-up business a very risky endeavor. Nevertheless, Jim believed it was still possible to reach his dream.

As a young engineer, he began researching the market possibilities to find a ground-floor opportunity around which to build a successful company. He believed he'd found such an opportunity when he discovered that Ford was taking bids to develop 10,000 small non-critical parts. With his keen eye for detail, Jim analyzed the requirements and specs and determined that he could design a more efficient process without compromising quality. This enabled him to submit a lower bid than the industry norm and still realize a healthy profit.

Jim quickly put together and submitted his bid, and after several meetings, Ford awarded Jim the contract. This resulted in a joint venture which grew to be a very large and successful brand in the automotive industry.

Not long after the business took flight, Jim and Evelyn made the decision to start a family. In time, they welcomed their first child—a precious baby boy they named Drake. Several years later, to their delight, Evelyn discovered they were expecting their second child. They welcomed Elizabeth, whose birth made their family of four complete. As Jim and Evelyn raised their two children, Jim continued to build a strong company. In fact, the enterprise grew far beyond their wildest dreams. So did Jim's financial portfolio.

In his later years, Jim's thoughts began to shift from how he could expand his business to how he could positively impact the lives of future generations. Like many people in his season of life, he began to ponder his legacy. And those thoughts brought him to my office.

Jim asked me several direct and specific questions. He wanted to know how to deal with his concerns regarding the future of the company—the succession of leadership and management, and how to best protect and provide for his wife and kids in the future. Beyond these important, practical financial matters, Jim was wrestling with even bigger questions—issues that transcended mere money.

Jim's concerns led me on a quest to discover the answers in their most transparent, most eternally meaningful form.

I have helped many families with their estate planning over a 25 year span. And in various forms, I've heard the legacy questions Jim asked repeated by others time and again. What continues to amaze me is the deep-seated impulse people have in the final chapters of their lives to finish well and to hand off to the next generation items of real value and lasting importance. This is much bigger than just the ancient ritual of passing the "stuff" on to heirs. That's really not such a hard task, although it does require some focus to work through the myriad of estate planning concepts currently available.

What I quickly learned in my unique role was that the most valuable and critical part of estate planning really doesn't have much to do with the "stuff" at all. I discovered that when the finish line in the race of life begins to come into view, our thoughts and hearts turn to bigger questions. We begin to wonder if we'll leave behind a legacy that will continue to have a positive impact on the world long after we're gone. This is a legacy that encompasses far more than money.

For years I successfully helped craft and carry out the final wishes of great family leaders by dealing with the "how" of estate planning. But the bigger, tougher issue is the "why." That question is at the heart of the book you now hold in your hands.

My calling compelled me to become a lifelong student of the principles (both practical and spiritual) of finishing well. Through my research, real-world experience, and revelation I have come to understand that no matter who you are, where you are in life, or what mistakes you've made in the past, it's possible to radically improve your future impact on those you love and the world they will inherit.

As I've talked with clients as they near the end of their lives, the conversations we've had have never been about diversification of assets, return on investments, or tax-minimizing strategies. Their last thoughts tend to have nothing to do with their "stuff" at all. They speak from their hearts and reveal what they consider to be their most treasured possession—their impact on the future.

Invariably, they speak of their desire to pass on to those they love an offering of themselves—their value systems, vision, and wisdom. They want to extend their blessings for safety, protection, and faith. They want to know they've helped equip the generations that follow to live good lives filled with purpose and productivity.

In other words, in those moments when what is truly important in life tends to come into sharp focus, family leaders think about leaving behind a legacy beyond money. And without exception, they wish they had started thinking about these things much sooner than they did.

No matter who you are; no matter your age; no matter what your net worth—it's time for you to begin thinking about these things, too.

My personal passion is to help you and others with that process. That's why I'm so excited that you've picked up this book. Creating a family plan gives your family purpose and vision. It establishes a firm foundation that impacts not only the relationships in your extended and immediate family but the lives of generations to come. This is the foundation on which your legacy is built.

As you will learn in the pages that follow, there is a difference between leaving a legacy, positive or negative, and passing a God-ordained heritage onto future generations. My hope is this book will guide you through the process of understanding the importance of legacy and heritage as well as guide you step-by-step through the process of how to develop them.

Transferring family wealth involves much more than just money. It includes passing forward emotional and spiritual purpose. And as you're about to discover, there is amazing power in determining, establishing, and communicating your life message to future generations. If you'll open your heart and mind, you'll receive everything you need to embrace your Heavenly heritage and establish a lasting legacy—a legacy that extends far beyond money or possessions.

CHAPTER ONE

HERITAGE VS. LEGACY

Lives of great men all remind us
We can make our lives sublime,
And, departing, leave behind us
Footprints on the sands of time.
— Henry Wadsworth Longfellow, <u>A Psalm of Life</u>

MOST OF US WANT to leave this world better than we found it. We want to leave a lasting impact on the lives of our families, friends, and others in our circles of influence. We want to leave behind a heritage of substance and value for the generations to come. This process is called "generational planning."

How exactly can we accomplish this goal successfully? While we cannot control the length of our lives, we can control the width and depth of our influence. We make a difference in the lives of others through the actions we take and choices we make each day.

In the chapters that follow, I am going to outline a process as well as provide the tools that will help you:

1. Determine and establish what values you desire to pass forward to future generations.
2. Recognize and evaluate the key relationships in your intentional circle of influence.
3. Clarify and create your family vision, mission, and purpose statements.
4. Understand and own the unique fingerprint God has given to your family that identifies who you are in Him.
5. Manage your "assets" (current assets, estate, tangible things of value) so they will be a blessing to future generations.
6. Create your own family life plan.

You may be asking yourself this question right about now: "What does generational planning have to do with understanding and embracing my God-given heritage or determining my personal legacy?" To answer this question, let's go back to the story of Jim and Evelyn that I began sharing with you in the "Introduction" pages of this book.

ONE FAMILY'S LEGACY

I first met Jim in the mid-nineties through a mutual colleague in the financial industry. Jim called to ask me if I would help him design a transitional family plan to guarantee the successful continuation of prosperity for future generations.

I walked into the first of what would be many meetings with Jim. Waiting to greet me was a large, robust man with dark hair and deep green eyes that penetrated directly into my soul. His warm smile revealed a kind heart and gentle nature.

After Jim took me on a private tour of the company, we returned to his office. Jim asked me the inevitable question, "What is your impression of the company?"

As I reflected on the building and the intricate machines, the first word out of my mouth was, "Impressive." Above all, I was impressed with the systemization, faithful staff, mutual respect, and strong leadership, which together created a highly competitive brand in his chosen marketplace.

The core of our conversation quickly turned to his unique business and personal opportunities. He shared with me how years ago he had been driven to grow the company and how he and Evelyn had experienced extraordinary financial blessing as a result.

At this stage in life, he was beginning to analyze the fruit of his labor, the life he had lived, and both the spiritual and financial blessings he and Evelyn had built. He looked me square in the eye and asked me a simple question, "How can I leave a lasting legacy as well as effectively transfer my assets when I die?"

HERITAGE VS. LEGACY

Jim's question is a common one. I hear it often as I help individuals walk through major life transitions and establish generational plans. My business is to help such outwardly successful people who don't fully understand or embrace the importance of successfully transferring a lasting legacy to future generations. In order to help them embrace the process it is first important to help them understand their God-given heritage. It is also important to help them understand that leaving a lasting legacy is about much more than just organizing the transfer of assets.

You may be asking yourself this question, as I asked myself for some time, "Aren't legacy and heritage the same things?" The answer is NO.

Your God-given heritage is yours by birthright, yet to receive it requires a decision on your part. It is a gift to open and accept, but to enjoy its fruits you must come into a personal relationship with God through faith in Jesus.

Your personal legacy, on the other hand, is determined by the values, traditions, and attributes that define who you are and that you pass forward from generation to generation. Your Family Legacy is the collective values, character, and attributes that define your family as a whole. For example, each finger along with your thumb has its own unique purpose when functioning separately rather than as a part of your hand. But when they function together, they form your hand. All four fingers and your thumb become one unit representing a common purpose rather than just five independent digits. It's the same when defining a family legacy. It is multiple individual legacies coming together to form one collective family legacy. How awesome is that?

Many family leaders are concerned about how their families will be taken care of after they are gone. If they are fortunate enough to have amassed a substantial estate, they often fret about who will eventually inherit their wealth. A father's concern over what he will leave behind— and who will inherit it—has been around for a very long time.

FAMILY HERITAGE AND GOD-GIVEN HERITAGE

Your family heritage is the link to your past. It gives you information about your lineage, the family line, from which you came. To simplify things, let's compare the generations that make up your family to an apple orchard. All families have their "good" and "bad" apples so to speak. Understanding your past helps you define who you are today and determine who you want or don't want to be tomorrow.

Have you ever visited an apple orchard in season? People come from all over to pick fresh apples. Each farm may grow a variety of apples, from Granny Smith to Golden Delicious, or Gala to Braeburn, among others.

Once you arrive at your orchard of choice, you grab a basket and head out to walk up and down rows and rows of trees scouring each branch for the best apples. At first glance, it may be difficult to identify the different types of apples growing from the trees just by looking at their shapes or colors. Some trees produce similar looking apples making it difficult to identify the type simply by looking at the physical characteristics of the apple. However, if you pick the apple from the tree, bite into it, and taste, it is easier to accurately determine its type. For example, Braeburn are firm and especially sweet, yet the similar-looking Gala is crisp and semi-sweet.

Some apples will be hard and not quite ready to pick. Others will be bruised or sour to taste. You examine the apples, carefully picking the best and leaving the rest. Once you have a full basket you are ready to head home and make a great tasting dessert.

Families are much the same. Each family has its own brand, its own unique signature … culturally, racially, spiritually, as well as the defined things each member values and holds out as important. The stories and experiences from one family to another are different as well. Add marriages and unions to the family orchard and then new trees sprout with their own unique shape, size, and fruit. From one tree to another, each family tree produces its own fruit. Healthy fruit intermixed with less healthy fruit.

As seasons come and go, year after year, the orchard continues to grow new trees. The trees that are pruned and well cared for produce more good fruit than bad. Those left to grow on their own will produce a very small amount of fruit deemed good enough to eat. And yet, the possibility for one good apple is always there as long as the tree has life.

In your family tree, you don't get to pick the tree from which your apple grows nor do we get to choose the orchard from which your tree initially sprouts. They choose you. You were born into a specific orchard and to a specific tree. However, you can choose who and what you individually become.

This brings us to your God-given heritage. While your family heritage is your link to the past, your God-given heritage is your link not only to the past but also to the future. Your God-given heritage is yours only through putting your faith in God. Faith is a choice, and it is your choice to make. God chose you from the very beginning of time. The truth is God was thinking about you long before you were thinking about Him. Through your life choices, both your family and your God-given heritage determine together not only the strength of your tree but the quality of the fruit your tree produces as the seasons of life come and go.

WHO'S YOUR DADDY?

Health Street is a mobile drug and DNA testing business. Their advertising slogan, "Who's Your Daddy?" appears in large letters on the side of their mobile lab trucks. The business kicked off in 2010, and within weeks of its launch, they had more demand than one mobile truck could handle. People stood in long lines to take a test that would solve mysteries about paternity and other family connections.

Why do you suppose this mobile start-up company did so well and grew so quickly in popularity? I think it is because people have a deep-seated need to know where they came from and to understand their true identity ... their DNA. Your God-given heritage also refers to your spiritual DNA. Be careful here to understand, your God-given Heritage is also a part of your Family Heritage and is not referring to your "spiritual family." Your spiritual DNA helps you understand who you are and why you do what you do.

To help you better understand the term spiritual DNA, let me tell you about Abraham. He was an old man when he began to worry about who would inherit his riches. But unlike my friend Jim, Abraham was childless. God had blessed him throughout his lifetime, but he had no son or daughter to pass his fortunes to. One hot afternoon, he found himself far from his childhood home sitting in the doorway of his tent under the shade of the oak trees. He sat scanning the horizon over the vast land he called his own.

We don't know what was going through Abraham's mind in that moment. I suppose Abraham was sitting in the doorway of his tent much like my grandfather sat in a rocker on a shaded Texas porch, lost in his own thoughts. Perhaps Abraham was reminiscing—remembering the days gone by. Maybe he was thinking about what life had been like prior to his own father's death. Possibly, he was contemplating the legacy he would one day pass to future generations and wondering how it would all come about.

What we do know is that later in the story, God did bless Abraham with a son and made him the father of many nations and of every generation to come thereafter. God sealed His covenant with Abraham, it is referred to as the Abrahamic Covenant, and it remains an everlasting covenant to this day, one that can never be broken.

You are in the direct lineage of Abraham. This means he is a part of your spiritual DNA; he is part of your spiritual heritage. We are heirs to the heritage of God through an irrevocable covenant He made with Abraham. How you receive it and choose to live it out, as well as what you do with it, is up to you. So ... Who's your Daddy? We will talk more about this and explore it in greater detail in the following chapters.

Understanding and embracing your God-given heritage will help you as you define and determine your legacy. This heritage is yours by birthright. Your parents have left you their legacy, and now you must determine the legacy your family will pass forward to future generations.

RECAP:

1. Leaving a lasting legacy is about much more than just securing the transfer of monetary wealth.
2. Your Family Legacy is defined by the collective values, character, and attributes that define your family as a whole.
3. We are in the direct lineage of Abraham, and he is the spiritual father of many nations.

CHAPTER TWO

DON'T STOP SHORT

"Our days are numbered. One of the primary goals in our lives
should be to prepare for our last day. The legacy we leave is
not just in our possessions, but in the quality of our lives."
— Billy Graham

YOU WERE CREATED TO accomplish great things. You are one
remarkable individual. You are called to have impact in all areas
of your life! Did you know that? The proof is found in the tips of your
fingers. You are the only person on Earth with your specific fingerprint.
That makes you unique.

No matter what your family tree and all the fruit on its branches may
look or taste like, you have the amazing opportunity to make a difference
in this world. To be a person of impact you must be purposeful in the
choices you make and how you manage your relationships with others in
your circle of influence, including your family, friends, career, community,
and church. The choice is yours as to what kind of impact you will have
today and pass forward to future generations.

Every person, experience, challenge, and victory from your past helped make you who you are. It isn't as much about what your past looks like as it is about how you choose to allow it to make you stronger and better. Understanding and embracing your past gives you the freedom to walk toward your future. Both your family and spiritual DNA give you the talents, gifts, and strengths that make you ... you.

Just as you have your own unique fingerprint and set of strengths, talents, and gifts, you also have a specific call on your life. Don't settle for less than God's perfect plan. You may be wondering, "Exactly how do I know what God's perfect plan is for my life? What does my call in life have to do with my past, present, and future?" Let's look again at the story of Abraham to help you find the answers.

EVERYONE IS CALLED TO SOMETHING

We left Abraham in chapter one sitting in the oak tree-shaded doorway of his tent, deep in thought. I suspect he was thinking about God's call on his life. You see, Abraham's father, Terah, started out following God's call as well. He set out to move the family from the corrupting culture of Ur to the more promising land of Canaan. But Terah stopped halfway along the journey settling in Haran instead. Terah and his family "set out from Ur of the Chaldeans to go to Canaan. But when they came to Haran, they *settled* there" (Genesis 11:31 NIV).

He never completed his God-given mission. Why do you suppose he stopped halfway? The Bible doesn't tell us. Maybe it was his health, the climate, or it's possible he was stopped because of fear. Perhaps he just got too comfortable where he was.

Terah's failure to complete God's ultimate call on his life did not change Abraham's calling. Abraham had respect for his father's leadership, but when Terah died, Abraham moved on to Canaan fulfilling God's ultimate call. He left his country, all of his relatives, and went to the place God showed him. There, God promised Abraham He would make him the father of a great nation, bless him, and make his name great. God also told him that every person would be blessed through his lineage going forward (Genesis 11-25).

It is important to know that sometimes God's call in life comes in stages. The time Abraham spent in Haran was a period of transition for him. He met and married his wife Sarah while there. It was also in Haran that Abraham received the words that established his obedient relationship with God. We see Abraham put his faith in God and we see God direct the faith of Abraham.

In the same way, God may give you times of transition and periods of waiting in your life as you move toward His call. It is in these times of transition that God helps you understand He is your lifeline. During the uncertain times in my own life, I find myself in a place where I must depend completely on Him for strength and trust my journey to His timing. If you will patiently do God's will during the transitional times in your life, you will be better prepared to serve God when He places His call on your life.

Now, like many guys, I'm a bottom-liner. Forget the fluff and just get to the stuff. And that's exactly how God communicated with Abraham. Basically, He gave Abraham three distinct commands to follow for moving on to Canaan and identifying and understanding his life-call: Go. Leave. Follow.

Go forth means to move onward, to **go** from one specific thing or place to another specific thing or place. It requires action on your part. *Go from* means to **leave** or let go of one thing in order to grab hold of something else. It requires surrender on your part or the willingness to let go of one thing in order to gain something else.

Go to means to move forward with intention, to **follow** after something. It requires an expected and anticipated outcome (vision) in order for you to move toward a specific destination.

As you set out to identify and understand your specific call in life, observe how Abraham surrendered and followed God's call in his life. I heard a saying that has resonated with me for some time especially in my line of work as a generational planner. "While the events of yesterday help in determining the direction of tomorrow, they can also hinder you from living your best today."

REAR-VIEW MIRROR

Yes, the past influences who we are in the present. I'll give you an example.

My parents taught me a strong work ethic from the time I was barely old enough to walk and talk. When I was eleven, I scored my first real job ... throwing a paper route in my hometown. Every day I picked up the papers from the newspaper office, rolled them one by one, put a rubber band around each, and off I went to throw the route. This was my daily work routine for several years.

By the time I was a freshman in high school, I was ready for greener pastures, literally. I traded my paper route for a job mowing grass. Living in the South, this was a very hot and dirty job, but I didn't care, it paid better.

After a few seasons of mowing yards, one yard stood out above all the others. It was the perfect yard, impeccably manicured with not a single weed in sight and at least three times greener than all its neighbors' yards. How those folks kept that yard so perfect amazed me so much so that I've never forgotten it. To this day, my own personal goal is to be the guy in my neighborhood with the perfectly manicured lawn. I dream about driving down my street and seeing that sign posted in front of my house that reads, "Yard of the Century."

I agree this story is a little excessive but my point is this: Your childhood, family, and life experiences, good or bad, have shaped you into who you are today—and who you are today determines how you will be remembered by future generations. You determine which parts of your past will be evident in your future by the decisions you are making now. I don't know what your past looks like, but I do know you have one. One thing we all have in common, like it or not, is a family history, but you do have a choice in what you decide to carry on to the next generation or bury—letting it end with you.

WHAT ARE YOU GOING TO DO
WITH THE PAST YOU'VE BEEN GIVEN?

To answer this question, let's look a little deeper at your Family Heritage, your family DNA. This DNA by its formal definition determines such things as your physical appearance, medical predisposition, intelligence, and even some personality traits. However, that's not all it defines. Your family DNA carries with it stories, history, and both good and bad relationships. It is these last aspects of your family DNA we are going to focus on now.

Whether you like it or not you share a connection to your parents, grandparents, and your ancestors going back many generations. These relationships have an impact on the life-choices you make, good, bad, and sometimes indifferent. Alex Haley, the author of *Roots*, writes, "The family is our refuge and our springboard; nourished on it, we can advance to new horizons. In every conceivable manner, the family is the link to our past, bridge to our future."

Just as God gave Abraham a specific call in life, you are given a specific call in life too. Theologian Frederick Buechner defines your life's call as being "the place where your deep gladness and the world's deep hunger meet." Had Abraham not pursued and obeyed God's call on his life, you would not be who you are today. You are the offspring of Abraham's obedience and his trust in a bigger plan. Through Abraham's covenant with God you are a part of a great nation whose blessings are available to you for the taking. Abraham passed forward an unbreakable covenant to every generation thereafter; you are the recipient of this call and blessing if you choose to receive it.

DEFINING YOUR FAMILY TREE

Let's take a minute and look at Abraham's family orchard. There are family trees grown by Adam and Eve, Cain, and Seth. Noah and Terah have their trees as well. When you look at the fruit from the trees, there are some good apples and some bad apples too. Some family members followed God and some family members didn't.

Abraham's dad, Terah, did not follow God's ultimate call on his life. Yet, God still blessed the wise decisions of the generations that followed in faith. When God first spoke to Abraham and told him to leave his homeland in Ur, God had already used Abraham's father, Terah, to begin the process (Genesis 11:31-32; Acts 7:4).

What God began with Abraham's father, he continued through Abraham's life and eventually completed through Abraham's descendants. If you'll remember, Terah only got as far as Haran. But Abraham later completed the family's journey to Canaan. Heritage can be a powerful factor in leadership. As in Abraham's case, God may begin a work in one generation and complete it through future generations.

Abraham did not come from generations of perfect people. His ancestors (Adam and Eve) took care of that! But what Abraham did do was follow God's call on his own life. He had amazing individuals within his family tree who chose good and right, yet he also had individuals who chose the opposite as their code by which to live. Yet, even with the undesirable trees that grew in his family orchard, Abraham chose to live a life of value and to pass forward a legacy of truth, goodness, respectability, hard work, and obedience deeply rooted in faith. These values revealed his family purpose and defined his family's character. Because of Abraham's decision to rise to God's call on his life, we share in his blessing.

Every orchard has its share of healthy trees with strong root systems growing very tasty fruit. Every orchard also has mixed among the healthy trees less than healthy ones with weaker roots growing little edible fruit. Whatever types of trees fill your family orchard, at any given time a tree can be nurtured or pruned. Diseased trees can even be treated and go on to recover and produce healthy fruit. You determine what you take with you from your past and what you pass forward to your future.

How you walk out the call on your life through the choices you make today will help shape your tomorrow. You were given by birth, through the covenant of Abraham, the opportunity to live a blessed life by choosing to pursue faith, honor, and obedience.

IMPACTING YOUR FUTURE

There are consequences to every choice you make, good and bad. Those consequences often extend wider than just your own life. So, you need to be intentional in taking up God's call on your life by living and managing today a legacy you are proud to pass forward to future generations.

Through each choice you make and action you live you are leaving fingerprints on the lives you touch. These fingerprints represent who you are, how others see you, and the legacy your future offspring will hopefully inherit. Your family DNA will impact future generations. Leave lasting fingerprints that represent Godly character.

If you desire to follow your call and define the fingerprint you pass forward, it is vital to embrace God's call on your life. And it is impossible to do this with an understanding of the core values and standards that come with that call. Through establishing your non-negotiable values you embrace how you are known, the standards you live by, the determining factors that direct your decisions, and the strong legacy you live out and pass forward.

It is also important to be intentional in the choices you make; you are called to a specific destination in your life. Don't settle for less than God's perfect plan. The greatest obstacle life throws at you is fear. Fear of failure and often times fear of success, but when you feel nervous, remember the flames of fear are extinguished through the power of faith. The choice is yours to make. Will you live a life limited by fear or intentionally by faith?

You were given the promise of abundant blessing by God at birth. To experience this blessing you must make wise choices and set goals in your life. Then, you must put energy behind your effort to reach these established goals. Your decisions today affect the generations of tomorrow.

RECAP

1. Just as you have unique fingerprints, talents, and gifts, you also have a unique and specific call on your life—to your family, your community, your church, and your profession—and it is all designed by God.

2. Whether you cherish the connection or not, you share a connection to your parents, grandparents, and ancestors that goes back for many generations. These relationships all have an impact on the life-choices you make whether those choices are good, bad, or indifferent.

3. You were given by spiritual birth, through the covenant of Abraham, the opportunity to live a blessed life by choosing to pursue faith, honor, and obedience.

CHAPTER THREE

EMBRACING THE CALL ON YOUR LIFE

"There's a calling for all of us. Every human being has value
and purpose. The real work of our lives is to become aware.
And awakened. To answer the call."
— Oprah Winfrey

FOR YEARS, ABRAHAM CLUNG to the words the Lord spoke to him after his father's death. Words of comfort and assurance, direction and purpose, words of promise and blessing, words Abraham never forgot. Abraham was called to **Go**, to begin moving from what he did yesterday toward a determined direction in his life, to **Leave** his comfort zone, and to **Follow** after God's call on his life for the future.

You have three specific time periods or days you experience in life, just as Abraham did. Your yesterday, which represents your "historical day," is full of both good and bad life experiences from the past. Your today represents your "now day," the things you do and choices you make over a 24-hour period. It includes the list of urgent and non-urgent matters you must accomplish so you will feel that your day was met with success. Your tomorrow is your "perfect dream day," that day where you will finally live out all the things you truly desire to accomplish.

Abraham was living his today when God showed up and placed His call on Abraham's life. Abraham was actually happy and content with the life he was living. But God had a bigger plan for Abraham's life.

If God called Abraham from his comfort zone of his today and toward a greater place for his tomorrow, do you think God can do the same for you? Does God really have a specific destination and plan for you? You betcha!

WE ARE CREATED TO DO GREAT THINGS

Let me tell you a little more about the life of Jim and Evelyn, the couple I introduced earlier. Jim and Evelyn followed God's call on their lives. Jim left the comfort of a stable job to set out on his own and build a successful company in the automobile manufacturing industry. He left the comfort of his yesterday, to begin something new with his today, in order to follow God's call on his life for tomorrow.

Jim was obedient and listened to God's direction in his life. He did his best to follow the path he was led to walk. He exercised integrity, honesty, and employed a hard-work ethic in everything he set forth to accomplish. Because he trusted God's leading, he followed God's call on his life with intention. Jim met great success in his life and amassed great blessing. Jim understood that the same call and promise God gave to Abraham, God also gave to him. It was Jim's heritage. A heritage he could not earn, but was his by birthright and therefore he could not lose it. This knowledge freed Jim and Evelyn to take on God's call for their lives and to find abundant success through their obedience to his call.

EVERY JOURNEY HAS ITS SIDE ROADS

Jim took great responsibility for everything regarding his business. That included demonstrating concern for the well-being of those working for him.

A few years after the busy couple welcomed their first child, Drake, Jim was met with an unexpected event at work one day. He went out to check on things in the warehouse and to encourage those working on the assembly line. These workers were a group of ladies working with small metal parts around a high-pressure hose. While looking around to survey the area he noticed something wrong with the line. He instinctively knew it was about to rupture. While yelling for the ladies to move away, he ran full speed toward the line and secured it with his bare hands.

Once he was sure everyone had made it a safe distance away he let go of the line. At that very instant the hose ruptured, badly injuring Jim's hands. Thankfully, his hands were not *on* the line as it blew, as the damage would have been so much worse. The doctors were successful in rebuilding his hands, but both were burned and bandaged for weeks. The pain was immense at times. When the line blew, tiny metal shavings embedded themselves into his hands and forearms. Jim never doubted God's call on his life even through this difficult circumstance. Over time his hands healed completely and he regained full function.

Jim's son was just eight months old at the time of the accident. But even with bandaged, painful hands, he held and rocked him for hours. Jim understood the things that truly mattered most in his life. He understood the importance of living a life of defined legacy for his children and working to pass forward a strong heritage.

It would have been easy for Jim to question his call in life through this obstacle and through other difficult circumstances that came his way. It would have been easy for him to throw in the towel and stop short of the goal when the days got long and opposition knocked at his door. Yet Jim chose to trust God's plan and purpose for his life no matter what. He determined "I will ... until ..." Once Jim accepted God's call on his life, stopping short was not an option.

UNDERSTANDING AND OBEYING THE CALL

Through my friendship with Jim I came to understand God was calling him and his family to something specific just as He did Abraham. And just as He does for you and me. God tells you in His Word, He knew you before you were born. He knew your innermost being and He knit you together in your mother's womb. What does this tell you? He knows your history, your yesterday; He knows your present, your today; and He knows your future, your tomorrow. How do you know you can trust God with your today and all your tomorrows? Because He was faithful to get you through yesterday!

God not only wants to meet you in your future but He wants to be with you every single step of the way. But what happens when we complicate things, and take the wrong side road rather than walking the straight path in life? Is it possible to miss the call?

To fully understand God's call in your life, you must understand relationship. God desires to have a relationship with you. God does not judge you against the actions of your past or the people who are a part of your past. When God looks at you He sees your potential, He looks past your mistakes and gives you everything you need to succeed in life. How does He do this?

In my life, I came into a relationship with God when I was eighteen years old while sitting in my dorm room in college. Four friends shared with me the value of surrendering my heart to God and believing that His Son Jesus died for my sins. They told me that God sent His Son Jesus to die on a cross for "my" sin, so I wouldn't have to. They said Jesus loved me right where I was and just as I was ... period. He covered the depths of my mistakes with His blood that was shed on the cross. All I had to do was ask for His forgiveness and give Him my life.

"That's it?" I asked. They said that was it, but it didn't mean that life would suddenly be easier. It meant when the difficult times came I would no longer walk through them alone. God would be with me and give me strength always.

From that day forward, I knew I had a personal relationship with God, one that continues today. I still deal with issues in my life. However, now, when hard times come, I deal with them from a place of hope rather than despair.

The moment I surrendered my way to God's way He began to change my self-centered attitudes and lifestyle. He has transformed the core of my heart from pursuing my way to seeking His way. It has been a process. Over time, I have learned to trust and rely more upon the truth that God promises to always protect and provide for me and my family.

Once you make the decision to **Go** into a relationship with God, and **Leave** behind the mistakes of your past, you will walk **Forward** by faith in God's grace every single day!

So, when you lay down your heart and take on God's heart, you find the call God created for you to fulfill. With God directing your journey there is nothing you cannot accomplish in life! To understand the call you must first know the one who is calling! However, to obey the call you must be willing to **Go**, **Leave** behind, and walk **Forward**.

GOODBYE YESTERDAY ... HELLO TOMORROW!

Don't let the things of yesterday hold your tomorrows captive! Just as Jim encountered obstacles and faced difficult circumstances on his journey to follow God's call on his life, so will you! We all have, do, and will. If you live in the Deep South as I do, you know what traveling on a farm-to-market road brings—slow-moving tractors, pot holes, and poor signage. These types of roads exist in our lives metaphorically too. We sometimes take them because we think they are going to be the short-cut to our destination only to realize what we forgot ... we knew better. Every time I do this I think to myself, "Guy, next time don't do this. Stick to the main road!"

In other words, we can learn from past mistakes. Taking a wrong turn doesn't mean you can't complete your call; it just means you need to re-evaluate the plan, realign your goals, renew your commitment, and refocus your energy.

Abraham was no different. Let's move on with his story and pick it up after God called him to continue the journey to Canaan. God told Abraham, "To your offspring, I will give this land" (Genesis 12:7 NIV).

Sometime later, when a famine hit the land, Abraham decided to go to Egypt so he could better provide for his family. As he was walking into Egypt he told his wife Sarah, "I know what a beautiful woman you are. When the Egyptians see you, they will say, "This is his wife." Then they will kill me but they will let you live. Say you are my sister, so that I will be treated well for your sake. And they won't kill me, which means you will save my life." (See Genesis 12:11-13.)

Abraham assumed that by telling a little white lie he could save his head from the chopping block. Sarah did what Abraham told her to do and was taken to live in Pharaoh's palace. But, God never misses a thing, He hears and knows everything. This lie angered God, so He brought disease onto Pharaoh and his family. Pharaoh uncovered the truth about Sarah, confronted Abraham, and told him to leave. Talk about hitting a bump in the road. Abraham probably made a mental note to himself, "Don't do that again!" In your life, what side roads or detours have you taken that have taught you valuable lessons? Are the lessons from yesterday shaping a better tomorrow for you?

GETTING BACK ON TRACK

Abraham packed up his family, his servants, all their possessions, and headed back to Canaan where he had pitched his tent in the first place before going to Egypt. Lot, his nephew, came back with him creating a problem. The land wasn't big enough to hold both of them.

Lot was like a brother to Abraham. So Abraham told Lot he didn't want to argue over who got what land or create issues between their herdsmen. He invited Lot to look over the whole land and pick any part of the land he wanted for himself first. Then he, Abraham, would take the half Lot left.

This offer to Lot from Abraham has always interested me. As the older guy, Abraham had the right to choose first, but instead he deferred to Lot. Maybe Abe was embarrassed about the way things went down in Egypt. Whatever the case, Lot did choose first. Guess what he chose ... greener grass. Yup, he looked at the land to his left. It was full of weeds, not as green, and needed work. But the land to the right looked perfect!

Lot looked up and saw the whole plain of the Jordan and noticed it was well watered and very green and healthy. So, he chose the best for himself and then he set out to live on this land.

Greener grass always looks perfect until you realize the price you have to pay to keep it green. The maintenance, chemicals, and effort it takes to pull and keep the weeds out just to keep it looking perfect can expend all the emotional and physical energy we should be putting into other more important things—things like pursuing God's call on our life, spending time with our families, or building positive relationships with others.

EMPLOYEE BENEFITS

As a business owner, I deal with three distinct issues on a daily basis: management, marketing, and production. In fact, all business owners deal with these same three issues across industry lines. On the management side, we face the task of hiring, training, and retraining good employees. One way we accomplish this goal is by putting a compensation plan in place that rewards the employee. We do this by offering a strong retirement plan option, good health and dental insurance, implementing a bonus program, and providing vacation days that reward the employees for a job well done.

Abraham was a good company man as well. God created employee benefits for him. When God called Abraham, He told him to "Go Forth," "Go From," and" Go To," and promised him that if he obeyed this call God would reward his obedience with a special bonus ... a gift that would keep on giving! What bonus, what gift, you ask? Let's look at it again:

> *I will make you into a great nation, and I will bless you;*
> *I will make your name great, and you will be a blessing.*
> *I will bless those who bless you, and whoever curses you*
> *I will curse; and all peoples on earth will be blessed*
> *through you.* –Genesis 12:2-3 NIV

Wow, talk about great benefits! I don't know about you, but I am definitely in! What an amazing gift. But exactly what does this mean for your life? Does this have an impact in defining and passing forward your legacy to future generations? We have established that God has placed a specific call on your life. He has a perfect plan with an exciting journey ending at the perfect destination.

On tough days, it may feel like you are all alone in your world of side-roads, pot holes, and hard-to-follow directions. But the truth is God is always beside you. He promises He will never leave you alone through the journey and He will never forget you in the journey! Life is full of its ups and downs and ins and outs, but at the end of the day, how you navigate the course and who you trust for direction is what will determine your ultimate destination. The key to embracing God's call on your life is laying down the choices and actions of yesterday before His cross of forgiveness, and walking forward through today and every tomorrow trusting Him to lead the way. You must choose to **Go**, **Leave** behind, and walk **Forward** through faith by grace. God is calling you, how will you answer?

RECAP

1. Taking a wrong turn in life doesn't mean you can't complete your call—it just means you need to reevaluate the plan, realign your goals, renew your commitment, and refocus your energy.
2. God desires to have a relationship with you; and you must get to know Him in order to better understand your call.
3. Greener grass always looks perfect until you realize the price you have to pay to keep it green.

CHAPTER FOUR

CHARTING AND
FINISHING THE COURSE

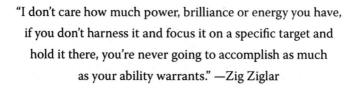

"I don't care how much power, brilliance or energy you have,
if you don't harness it and focus it on a specific target and
hold it there, you're never going to accomplish as much
as your ability warrants." —Zig Ziglar

I WOKE UP EARLY on a bright Saturday morning in the spring of 1975
to celebrate another milestone ... my sixteenth birthday. I started
the day thinking about my upbringing surrounded by my four siblings
and determined it was they who had more than prepared me for the
presentation I was about to give. I was a clean-cut kid living in a world of
change during the seventies. As I entered the kitchen in my house there
stood the gateway to my new found freedom, my mother. She seemed
calm, cool, and collected as she put away the breakfast dishes. Being the
youngest of five kids I knew how to turn on the charm. I got my mother's
attention, positioned myself just right and began my well-rehearsed pitch.

I used my creative energy and unwavering resolve as I began my oratorical masterpiece. I first thanked my mom for the wonderful job she and dad had done in raising me. I pointed out the strong work ethic they had instilled in me and expressed my deep appreciation for the example they had set and how it would benefit me as I began my new summer job. I continued my presentation by informing her of the sheer excitement I felt each time we camped out as a family at the nearby lake. Then, I casually and with great smoothness transitioned to the coming school year pointing out how busy I was going to be with sports and working my part-time job.

Feeling I had created an aura of positive vibes, I closed the presentation with, "And due to the time constraints I will face this fall, I have decided to drop out of Boy Scouts." I paused, waiting for her response. She quietly finished putting away the dishes, set the dishtowel on the countertop, and asked me to follow her to the kitchen table. We sat down together and she calmly asked me a simple question, "Guy, why do you want to do that when you are so close to earning your Eagle Scout?"

Before answering her question I thought back on my journey through Boy Scouts of America. I was encouraged to join scouts by watching my older brother's journey into the ranks of scouting and observing the benefits he received from the campouts, as well as the experiences and camaraderie he enjoyed with the other guys.

My journey in Scouts started in grade school when I joined Cub Scouts. Over the course of a few years I completed the highest rank and graduated on to Boy Scouts. I attended the weekly meetings and looked forward to the monthly campouts. Within our "troop" we divided into several "packs" of boys who joined forces and grew through the program together. We worked in unison to prepare meals and set-up our campsite using timber and rope to build ovens, tables, and fences.

We all became chefs in our own right as we learned how to cook our version of a gourmet meal using seasoning, aluminum foil, Dutch ovens and hot burning coals to make roast, cobbler, homemade biscuits, and a breakfast to die for. We used the daytime on these campouts to work on completing our merit badges, and one step at a time, I worked up the ladder from Tenderfoot, to Star, to Life, and finally I was moving toward achieving the highest possible rank in Boy Scouts, the Eagle Scout Award.

My thoughts were interrupted by my Mom's voice as she repeated her question again. In truth the real reason I wanted to quit and eliminate scouting from my future was my new girlfriend and my desire to accelerate my high school sports career. I had observed that none of the "cool" upper classmates participated in scouting at my high school and I was all about being chosen by the "in crowd" at this stage in my life. I reiterated my reasons for wanting to quit—a new job, sports activities, and school work (notice my savvyness in keeping the girlfriend out of the picture). Mom nodded and after a long silence she said she would discuss everything with my dad later and then we would talk together about the decision.

I was very impressed with my presentation and satisfied that I had made a strong case in favor of my desired outcome. The next morning I joined my parents at the breakfast table where the discussion continued. My father was a great man who had learned when to defer to my mom's wisdom in matters of the family. That day I learned that no matter how well you do in a formal presentation, there is always someone who will do better!

Dad began the discussion by pointing out the benefits of completing the Eagle Scout Award. He noted that numerous world leaders, con- gressman, senators, governors, astronauts, and corporate CEOs had completed their scouting experience earning the prestigious award. Among them were Neil Armstrong, who left an indelible mark on mankind by being the first man to leave his footprint on the moon, and Gerald Ford, who was vice president at the time and widely known for his integrity. He cited other high achievers and each had one thing in common. They completed their Boy Scout journey by earning Scouting's highest prize.

Mom pointed out that Scouting was instilling within me strong char- acter and discipline that would benefit my entire life, my future family, and my eventual career. When they finished talking with me, my desire to move on to other pursuits seemed trivial. I listened to their wisdom and guidance that morning and made the decision to finish the course I had charted in Scouts.

In the weeks that followed I completed my last four merit badges; determined, organized, and finished my community project; and received my Eagle Scout Award in the fall of that year.

This process helped to shape my personal character as well as helped me to understand the importance of cooperation and service toward my church, home, school, community, and friends. It aided me in establishing the right attitude toward God, and that is the anchor which holds me down to this day.

There are three main parts to the Scout Oath that I've carried with me through life and try to live out each day. "I will do my best to do my duty first to God and country, second to other people by helping them at all times, and third to myself by keeping me physically strong, mentally awake, and morally straight." These are components of my purpose statement in life, as it defines who I am, what I will do, and where I am going.

My history—the sum of my past experiences—has shaped and influenced the life I live today. As I reflect on many conversations with my parents over the years, I see how right they were in their wisdom. Pursuing the call and finishing the course in Scouts and ultimately earning the highest award continues to have impact in the choices I make, the values I walk out, and the determinations I make.

Looking back I would have quit my journey through Scouts in a heartbeat had my parents not reminded me of the value of staying the course and obeying the call. By encouraging me to visualize my future, they provided me with needed guidance. The impact of my decision to follow their lead made all the difference in my life from that point moving forward. Because of their influence in my life I stayed the course. Today, I find myself working to instill those same guidelines and non-negotiables in the lives of my own children.

DEFINING MOMENTS

We all have defining moments in our lives. Each major life event from your past that caused a turning point in your life's journey is a defining moment. Think of it this way: Your life is like a timeline. The first point of interest marks the place you were born.

Moving forward, life is full of experiences, major events in your life that influence the direction you take and accomplishments you make. With each experience a mark is placed on the timeline. These events may be positive or negative but they may have created a change in the direction you were going. There won't be an abundance of them, but looking back they left an indelible mark in your mind. It was at this point that the course of your life was altered, your direction changed in some way.

My personal journey through Eagle Scouts and my decision to persevere still helps to define my life today. That is one of my defining moments. If you looked at my map you would see this point clearly marked.

For some, a defining moment in your life may be a major illness, a divorce in your family, the death of a parent or loved one, it may be a distinct change, good or bad, in your family economics. It may be a move from one state to another, or even a transfer from one school to another. These life experiences represent both the positive and negative events from your past. Looking back, you can say without a doubt it was at this point that a definable change occurred in my life. It changed my direction; it shaped my perceptions moving forward, and it became a defining moment.

Identifying these moments from your past will help you as you discern why you are where you are today and walk out your current call in life. It helps you in determining if the events in your past derailed the course you were traveling leaving you somehow stuck in a place unable to move forward. You may find the opposite true as well, the events in your past spurred you onward toward walking out the call God placed on your life.

How you embrace or let go of these defining moments determines much about how you live out the future. Everyone tends to internalize stuff. It is how you choose to deal with your stuff, both good and bad, that either makes you better or bitter. Difficulties can become your greatest springboards in life. It is all about what you do with what you are given and how you use it to become stronger.

A DEFINING MOMENT FROM ABRAHAM'S PAST

When God places a call on the life of a family leader, and that leader doesn't listen to the directive, what really happens? Do that leader's decisions really have an impact on future generations?

Let's go back and look again at Terah's decision to stop north in Haran instead of completing the journey by going west to Canaan. Terah had a vision for Canaan but settled for Haran. Had he continued on to Canaan would things have looked differently for his family? They would have arrived in Canaan before the great famine and established themselves there in the land and maybe they never would have ended up as they did living in the midst of a corrupt Egypt. Whatever the case might have been, God eventually called Abram (as Abraham was known at this time) to leave his home in Haran and complete the call of God by continuing the journey to Canaan.

Whatever the past influences on Abram as he grew up in the house of his father Terah or the events that occurred on his journey toward Canaan, one thing is clear, God used these defining moments in Abram's life to continue the family's legacy. Terah settled, but Abram did not. What about you? Have you settled for less than God's best in your life? Have circumstances or even fear kept you from moving forward toward accomplishing God's call on your life? Are you sitting in Haran with a vision of Canaan?

After Terah's death, God's call on Abraham's life was evident. God's promise to walk the journey alongside Abraham established a covenant that would bless all nations and future generations to come. We are a part of Abraham's legacy!

What can we learn from this story? The decisions we make today can and do have great impact on future generations. We see how the defining moments of our past help to shape the decisions of our present and future. We see that we don't have to surrender to the bad influences in our lives but rather can use them as a springboard to a better life today and a legacy of brighter tomorrows for our heirs.

Abraham grew up surrounded by the worship of false gods yet in spite of these influences he chose to worship the one true God. This one decision changed the course for every generation to come. Even though his father, Terah, may have stopped short of completing God's call, Abraham did not let Terah's decisions derail his obedience to God's call on his life.

Look back now over your own life. Can you identify some defining moments? As the leader in your home, your company, and within your circle of influence you are establishing your legacy through the everyday decisions you make and you are affecting the lives of those around you. Are you pleased with the legacy you were handed by those who came before you? If those who handed down your family heritage chose destructive side-roads or passed forward a negative legacy, please remember that you have another heritage that is your birthright. It is through this DNA that you establish your new legacy. You have a Heavenly Father who will not abandon you and who has a perfect plan for your life! If you don't know the plan, ask the Planner!

RUN BABY RUN!

In junior high and high school it seems every kid is trying to fit in, stand out, or just survive those years. I was no different when I was in high school. I desperately wanted to be a successful athlete by excelling in sports. The first sport I played was basketball. I played a respectable game and at least did not embarrass myself on the court. Eventually though, I moved on to track. I found I had potential in track and ran the 800 and 1600 meter events. Back in my day it was called the 880 and the mile. To this day I can still feel the burn in my legs as I crossed the finish lines. My dream was to be a sprinter. However, I was not blessed with the speed to accomplish this goal. So I ran the mid-distance to the best of my ability and earned my team some points in the process.

Do you remember an Olympian named Derek Redmond? He was favored to win the gold in the 400 meter run for Team Britain in the 1988 Olympics in Seoul, Korea. He was lightning-fast and ran like a gazelle with perfect form. He set the 400-meter British record in 1985 with a time of 44.82 and again in 1987 with a time of 44.50. He held this record until it was broken in 1992.

At the 1988 Olympics in Seoul, an injury to his Achilles tendon forced him to pull out of the opening round of the 400 meter run 90 seconds before his heat was due to begin. Over the next year he endured eight operations due to injuries. Nevertheless, he was determined to recover and compete in the 1992 Olympics in Barcelona, Spain, and earn a medal. The color of the medal no longer mattered to Redmond. He wanted to finish the race he had trained to run over his lifetime. He knew this Olympics would be his last chance to compete in the 400 meter run as he was aging and injuries were taking their toll on him.

Redmond was in good form by the time the Barcelona Olympics arrived. On the morning of the race, Derek visited with his dad, Jim, about his past failures and heartbreaks throughout his years of competition. They both agreed that it was important for Derek to perform at his best and finish the race in this final competition, as a tribute to all the hard work he'd put in to recovering and training for this day.

Derek posted the fastest time of the first qualifying heat and went on to win his quarter-final. In the semi-final, Derek shot out of the blocks and established a clear lead coming out of the first turn. But a few seconds later, in the back straight, about 250 meters from the finish, his hamstring snapped. He hobbled to a halt, and then fell to the ground in intense pain as the stadium spectators gasped and millions of television viewers stared in disbelief. Stretcher bearers rushed onto the track, but Derek remembered the talk he had with his Dad earlier that day. To the shock of every observer, he struggled to his feet and began hobbling and hopping toward the finish line. A television camera searched in vain to find Derek's father where he had been sitting in the stands encouraging his son toward the finish line. Jim was already out of his seat, running down the stairs toward his son.

Derek's father pushed past Security and onto the track to get to his son. Jim whispered in Derek's ear, "I'm here son, we will finish together." The pair completed the final stretch of the race side by side, with Derek leaning on his father's shoulder for support. Just before they crossed the finish line, Jim let go of Derek allowing him to cross on his own. The crowd of 65,000 spectators rose to their feet to give Derek a standing ovation.

However, because his father had stepped onto the track, Derek was officially disqualified and Olympic records state that he "Did Not Finish" the race. The viewers that day know what the records do not show. Derek Redmond finished his race that day.

Derek learned on this day, as all of us do, that there will be setbacks in our lives. How we choose to handle them is what forms who we are, what we become, and the moments that will define us. As I reflect on this story tears fill my eyes. For me, the greatest image was not just Derek's courage but that he had a father who was there for him when he needed to finish the race.

You have a Heavenly Father who will go the distance with you and walk beside you every step of the way as you finish the race you are called to run. When obstacles come, and they will, he will not leave you to run alone; rather he will give you everything you need to cross the finish line and claim victory!

Derek understood the call on his life. He focused his eyes on the prize and trained to that end. When obstacles came he found a way to rebound, recover, and redirect his attention toward accomplishing the goal and completing the call. That year, Derek didn't win an Olympic medal as was anticipated by those who competed against him. But Derek finished the race. He fixed his eyes on the call, he leaned in to his dad for strength when his strength was gone, and he won the greatest prize of all ... he completed the call. He could have stopped short and no one would have blamed him, but he didn't, and in so doing he demonstrated for the world what courage looks like. One choice, one moment, defined his legacy. He chose to finish the race set before him.

Today's decisions impact tomorrow's reality. For better or worse, they create your future legacy.

THE WORTHIEST CALL

The leader of the family is the one who shoulders the responsibility to provide vision, direction, and comfort for present and future generations. God's call for each of us is specific and unique, but not everyone accepts his or her call. Creating the foundation of generational planning begins with visualizing a future that is communicated both verbally and in writing. It must be tempered with the knowledge that all the decisions made today can and will affect all the generations to come.

Measuring the success of your family's planning becomes vitally important as you evaluate where your family is right now in the midst of this journey. It's okay to change your goals or your direction but only through measurement can we determine how effective the leadership is in impacting the future of the family.

The words Jim spoke as he grabbed hold of his son on the track in Barcelona need to ring loudly in our ears as well, "I am here son, and we will finish together." What encouraging words from an earthly father to his son. God speaks these words to you each and every day. All you have to do is ask and God will carry you the distance and across the finish line.

RECAP

1. Identify the definable moments in your life and how they have been a key factor in charting your course up to this point.
2. The decisions we make today can and do have great impact on future generations.
3. Finishing well is important in transferring your legacy as the next generation prepares to run its race.

CHAPTER FIVE

LEGACY:
DEFINING VALUE AND
DETERMINING WORTH

"Try not to become a man of success. Rather become a
man of value." —Albert Einstein

WHAT DO YOU VALUE in life? At some point along your life's journey you began to define your value as a person. How you value yourself also determines the worth you place on both the tangibles and intangibles of your past, present, and future. What you value shapes your legacy. And the views and values of those in your lineage going back for generations played a role in shaping who you are today.

In order for you to define the nature of the legacy you pass forward you must first understand your worldview. It is important for you to determine and establish your non-negotiable values and defined self-worth. You begin by evaluating your past.

SELF-WORTH GONE AWRY

I clearly remember a particular day in February of 1973. I was thirteen and in the eighth grade, a pivotal year for any student. One morning in gym class I started feeling sick and my coach sent me to the nurse's office. The nurse took my temperature and discovered it was high. She sent me on to my English class and called my parents to come pick me up.

What happened in the first moments after I walked into my classroom made a powerful and lasting impact on how I viewed and valued myself. It also impacted the importance I would one day come to put on "stuff" as it related to my personal sense of worth. From this day forward for many years to follow, I would allow the opinions *of others to determine my sense of personal value.*

As I sat down, the popular cheerleader and star athlete decided it was my turn to experience the power of being cut-down—*bullied* is the word today. They both proceeded to make fun of what I was wearing. They talked so loud that everyone around me could hear. No, I didn't wear the coolest clothes. And if that wasn't bad enough, I had just hit puberty—growing four inches in a matter of months. All my pants were considerably shorter than was fashionable. My family was blue-collar by current standards, so I used the money I made throwing an afternoon paper route to buy clothes for myself.

As they continued launching negative comments at me, I resorted to my tactic of playing as though I didn't hear what was being said. The bullying continued, and I was made painfully aware that I was not, never had been, nor ever would be a part of their "cool crowd." Five minutes into this ordeal, a voice blared over the loud speaker saying, "Guy, your mom is here."

The sneers and snickers increased as I got up from my seat and walked toward the door. I finally reached the exit and I made a fierce, solemn vow to myself: "Someday, no one will ever be able to make fun of who I am or what I have."

That experience planted the seed in my mind that "stuff" carried enormous value in life. That seed concept grew into a life built around a negative and self-centered value system. I would battle that distorted viewpoint for many years to follow and well into my adult life. The humiliation I experienced at school that day left a scar on my heart that is still visible today.

So how did the inner vow I made as I left class that day change how I valued myself? At that moment, I chose to accept the opinions of others as the true measure of my value. And the way I valued myself and everything around me began to drive my definition of success.

With that view, I began to value myself by the size of my house, the type of car I drove, the jewelry I purchased for my wife, the clothing labels my family and I wore, my career, social status, and my annual income. The fallacy with this value system is that there is never enough and you are never enough, and the world keeps changing the rules. What is deemed as treasure—a must-have sign of success today—will all be defined differently tomorrow.

The result of these choices was that I looked to *the wrong things and the wrong people* to give value to my life and fulfill my emotional needs. It wasn't until I admitted to myself that the way I was measuring my value was not only wrong but did not honor God that I began to understand and own a biblical concept of true acceptance: "Who I am is tied directly to my relationship in Christ, who died for me, and nothing else and nothing more ... period."

Today, I understand the real truth of who I am. Any success I have achieved is through God alone. I deserve nothing in and of myself, but, in and through a perfect God who *is* my motivation for everything. People and things do not determine our value or worth ... God does. He says "we are more than enough."

LIVING LIFE AS THE JONESES

We've all heard the saying, "They are just trying to keep up with the Jones." Who the heck are the Joneses? And what do they have that is so worth keeping up with? If you ask me, Mr. and Mrs. Jones are responsible for creating a culture of lust and desire drawn directly from the world's concept of success.

The world says pursue wealth and then you will be happy, pursue youth and you will have many friends, move to a bigger house and drive a better car, then you will have arrived. More, more, and more stuff is not going to satisfy an empty soul. You will just be an empty person with more stuff.

Does anyone know if the Joneses were content in their lives? Did they have peace? Were their days filled with joy and purpose? I have often wondered if we lived our lives as if "we" were the Joneses and set a responsible example for others to follow how would that change not only how we live our lives but how our circle of our influence live theirs. I am sure of one thing, I would not want to be a member of the Jones' generational heritage nor would I want to receive their legacy.

My career has allowed me to interview and help numerous wealthy families. Let's look again at my friends, Jim and Evelyn. You learned in earlier chapters how they acquired their financial wealth. Yet more importantly, take note of how they viewed their wealth and to what (or whom) they credit their success in building their wealth.

Jim and Evelyn understood very early in their lives that God was the source of all they had. However, looking to God to determine their value and to direct His call on their lives was a process that played out, in all honesty, over time. God ushered them to the place where they fully understood He was the absolute source of all their blessings. Over time and through the highs and lows of life they learned what it meant to find complete contentment through a relationship with God rather than searching for contentment in money.

Through several years of working with Jim on establishing a generational plan prior to his death, the following principle became very clear to me. More than leaving monetary worth, Jim desired to leave a lasting legacy that championed a Christian worldview and a God-inspired value system. He understood that before one can properly value stuff, one must properly value the self. This comes from looking into God's mirror to determine self-worth and self-value rather than looking into man's mirror.

How about you, are you content with who you are, where you are, and what you have in life? Whose mirror are you looking into to determine your self-worth and self-value? Looking outward for value and acceptance will never satisfy the human soul—learn from my experience in high school. Peace and hope are found when you see yourself as the God who created you sees you ... perfectly and wonderfully made complete in His image from the very beginning of life!

TRANSFERRING A LOT OF VALUE FORWARD

Let's look back at Abraham again. Abram, as Scripture continues to refer to him at this point, had amassed large flocks of sheep, cattle, and male and female donkeys. Along with his herds he also employed many men and maidservants to tend to all the things he had acquired. One could say he had amassed great monetary wealth.

The main thing that set Abram apart from other men, kings, and rulers of great wealth during this time was—even though Abram had lots of stuff or worldly possessions—His eyes never left the source of his blessings ... God. Abram "fixed" his eyes on God and understood that He was the ultimate source of his call, his faith, and all his possessions. His value came from God and he walked it out through the power of God.

Abram actually acquired much of his wealth from the same Pharaoh who took Sarah as his wife. Remember the "little white lie" from the earlier chapter? Pharaoh was not aware he had married the wife of Abram, he thought she was Abram's sister. God decided to rectify this problem by inflicting Pharaoh's household with some serious diseases. As soon as Pharaoh was made aware he had taken another man's wife into his palace, he immediately made amends. He not only sent Sarah back to Abram, but also gave Abram a great amount of tangible wealth in the form of livestock, as well as the servants to care for them. "He treated Abram well for her sake, and Abram acquired sheep and cattle, male and female donkeys, menservants and maidservants, and camels" (Genesis 12:16 NIV).

From there, Abram's wealth continued to grow in gold and silver as well. "Abram had become very wealthy in livestock and in silver and gold" (Genesis 13:2 NIV).

God had already blessed Abram by giving him the land, and now He was adding a great amount of physical assets to that blessing through Pharaoh.

So was Abram's wealth built from the fruit of his labor or just because God blessed him? Actually, it was both; he received God's blessing and was a faithful "steward" in how he managed the wealth he was given. His view was proper in how he received his wealth, and he eventually transferred that wealth to his son Isaac. Abraham recognized that he did not "own" anything but was merely the steward of all God's blessings.

I want you to understand clearly that God chooses to bless some individuals with great monetary wealth, and when He does, He also places high expectations on how the wealth is managed and used to bless others. Having money is not bad, hoarding money is. It is about living out the mindset, "I will give from that which I have been given. At the end of the day blessing of any kind is not only mine to enjoy 'from' God it is mine to give 'for' God.

Abraham not only left his entire estate to Isaac, more importantly, he handled the rest of his legacy just as efficiently. He gave gifts throughout his lifetime to other sons born to him by his maidservants.

Abraham dealt with his family's heritage, relationships, values, and vision before he dealt with his "stuff" or assets. He acted upon God's blessing by trusting his lineage would continue through Isaac alone. This act protected Isaac from jealous siblings and is a great example of a patriarch (family leader) who has the courage to cast his God-given vision upon his family. In turn he provided a legacy of wisdom for future generations to follow.

This isn't the case for many seemingly successful people. Many leave a legacy of loose ends and unsolved problems.

UNFINISHED BUSINESS

When families and individuals leave behind unfinished business the living are left to work through unresolved issues. This scenario can be avoided by managing your "tangible stuff" well and making transitional decisions from a deeply-rooted, value-driven mindset. Being a good "steward" of the "stuff" God has given you means planning well and distributing well God's blessings and resources.

One scenario I have seen occurring often within families is unresolved perceptions of value and worth, which come to light after the death of a loved one. The children did not receive the affirmation they needed from their parents and are now transferring that unmet need into fighting over the "stuff" left behind. It really isn't about the cash or things; it is all about what the cash or things represent. In other words, it's really about unmet emotional needs rather than physical needs. It is about an innate need God planted within each of us from the moment we were created to know and receive a spiritual and emotional heritage.

You may be wondering how you can avoid this scenario in your family. It begins with the implementation of our faith. Understanding God has called us to pass forward the emotional and spiritual heritage He planted in the depths of our hearts. However, the process takes time, so don't wait until it's too late. On the up side, it is absolutely possible to plan in such a manner to positively empower rather than negatively impact future generations.

IT'S NOT ABOUT YOU, BUT ALL ABOUT ME!

Your life, to this point, has been filled with experiences and relationships that shaped you into who you are today. At the very core of your being, you must define for yourself what is really valuable. No one can do it for you.

This process is made easier if you have a framework of reference from which to work. This is where a family plan comes into play. When you help your children understand the values on which you stand and why, you are guiding them toward an "others"-motivated mindset and away from a "self"-motivated mindset.

From that, you begin to establish the legacy you desire to pass forward to your family and future generations. When you understand the core of your value rests in none other than God's opinion of you, you will be an influencer in establishing the same perspective for the other members within your family unit. As you, the family leader, walk out a God-defined and God-determined sense of worldview and world-value you will empower your spouse, your children, and others to follow your lead. In turn, your family will have major impact on and create value in the lives of others.

As the leader of your family, you hold the towel of influence. Some leaders go around waving their towels while others get frustrated and throw in their towels. The best leaders wrap their towels around their waists, and wash the feet not only of those in their immediate circles of influences but within their families too. It is called Servant Leadership. Sometimes the most difficult people you will ever be called to serve or influence are those within your own family unit. However if you aren't willing to lead the ones closest to you how can you possibly think you can lead the masses?

Abraham understood this principle well. He led by example. Did Lot follow the same value system of Abraham without wavering? No he didn't. And he paid a great price for going his own way. Both Abraham and Lot were equal from a possession standpoint, they owned equal parts of land, herds, and were even followed by equal numbers of people. Yet, while many followed Abraham out of Ur and into the land of Canaan, no one followed Lot out of the land of Sodom and Gomorrah. Why? Those who followed Abraham saw the Godly legacy of the man unfold before their very eyes; those who watched Lot walk away saw no legacy to follow.

How you honor the generations before you will come back around in the manner in which your children honor you. How you manage the stuff you are handed is making an impression on the lives of your kids. "Train up a child in the way he should go, and when he is old he will not depart from it," (Proverbs 22:6 NKJV). Teach honor and respect.

Before you can be an effective leader of your family you must be an effective follower of God in *all* things. You teach what you know and reproduce who you are. The fruit of your efforts will grow on the trees of those you influence.

RECAP:

1. Your world values shape your legacy, and they will influence those who come after you. Your ancestors have played a role in how you perceive the world around you, just as you will play a role in distant heirs you will never meet.
2. Pursuing the world's definition of value will only leave you feeling empty inside.
3. Abraham had lots of stuff, yet he recognized his true source of value was God.

CHAPTER SIX

THE NAME BEHIND YOUR FAMILY BRAND

"A good name is more desirable than great riches; to be esteemed is better than silver or gold." —Proverbs 22:1 NIV

Names are important. They have power. They represent much more than just a collection of letters that sound good and identify a person. Names were not created merely as a way to make it easier for us to communicate with each other. Names are a gift from God. They don't just identify us, they define us. A name can be a destiny.

In the beginning of creation when God ordered light into the world He also named it into existence. He did the same with darkness, the sun, moon, stars, and man. He could have left us all simply known as "man and woman," but He didn't. He gave the first man and woman specific names … Adam and Eve. Not only did He name them, He attached meaning to their names. Adam means "from the earth." Eve means "the mother of all." This shows the importance God places on names and what they represent. God created branding!

When I was born, my mother and father gave me a name—Randy Guy Hatcher. Randy means "esteemed for courage." Guy means "leader/ warrior." Hatcher identifies me as belonging to a specific patriarchal line. While doing research for this chapter, I called my mom and asked her exactly why she and Dad gave me my specific two names.

She explained that my uncle Guy was the second of my grandparent's ten children. My dad was the youngest. One July 4th, years before I was born, my uncle Guy lost a battle with cancer. His untimely death devastated the family so deeply they never again celebrated the July 4th holiday. They couldn't bare the memories that day brought. Mom said she thought the name Guy was precious because it represented the much-older brother my dad loved and looked up to. Randy was a name my parents just liked and they thought the meaning fit well.

I am the youngest Hatcher kid. I have one older brother and three older sisters. Mom said she and Dad knew from the day they found out she was pregnant with me I would be their last child. They both felt God had big plans for my life. So, they wanted me to have a strong name. Mom said in many ways my birth and name brought some healing and joy to my Grandparents and to my dad. So you see, names are important. They contain meaning. They are powerful and define who we are.

YOUR NAME DEFINED

Over time, your name picks up additional meaning. What it gathers is called your *reputation*. When those who know you hear your name, their minds instinctively paint a mental picture of what you look like on the outside and what you represent on the inside. Are you a person others respect? What values do you represent each day as you walk out your life? What do you stand for? What ideas, thoughts, and images do you think pop into another person's mind the minute they hear your name?

Your character determines your reputation. One way your character is defined is summed up with the following question: Who are you when no one is looking? Let's have a little fun here as a way to drive this point home. I will mention a few names and you think about what attributes come to mind as you visualize and define each person. Bill Gates. The Pope. Michael Jackson. Donald Trump. Jesus Christ. Billy Graham. Martin Luther King Jr. Adolph Hitler.

Each person on that list is unique. Several may share similar values, attributes, or accomplishments, but each one has established his own specific brand, good or bad. The name, action, and life choices built an image in the minds of others. This image is a message that says, "This is who I am and this is in whom and what I believe."

THE FAMILY NAME: A DEFINING FORCE

Your "family name" is also synonymous with the legacy you are establishing as you walk out your daily life. As the leader of your family, you have a lot to do with defining what your family name represents. When others hear your last name or your surname, what attributes or character traits do they associate with your name?

Remember the family orchard I mentioned earlier? Your extended family brand represents the orchard as a whole. However, as each child leaves home, a new tree takes root and a new immediate family tree is established. Each branch on the tree represents an individual within the family.

Your spiritual heritage largely determines the strength of your tree's root system. Everything that grows out of those roots gives the tree its firm foundation. Nurtured well with the right amount of water and sunlight, your tree's root system will grow deep and strong producing lots of healthy and vibrant fruit. However, in the absence of adequate water and sunlight, the tree's root system will grow shallow and weaker roots that produce less healthy, vibrant fruit.

Now, let's try the same name-association exercise we did earlier in driving home the importance of establishing a strong family identity, only this time let's use only surnames. I will mention a few names and you think about what attributes come to mind as you visualize and define these families. The Kennedys. The Rockefellers. The Royal Family. The Jacksons, and the Joneses.

In doing this exercise myself, I discovered that as I visualized these families a few individuals influenced how I perceived the entire family. However, when I separated them into separate family units within the whole, I realized each individual family had its own unique characteristics. Breaking it down further, each person within a specific family had his/her own individual character fingerprint. I found it interesting how I instinctively made these observations and distinctions upon just hearing a name.

As you begin the process of establishing your family legacy, think about this question. Within your home, is the character and value system your name represents important enough to you to develop, protect, and defend it?

ABRAHAM'S FAMILY BRAND

Just as God branded Adam and Eve, He likewise branded Abraham as the "father of all nations." Twelve tribes were established through the lineage of Abraham, each tribe carried a collective brand under the Abrahamic Covenant as well as an individual brand. Sound familiar ... think back to the family orchard! As a matter of fact, you are a spiritual descendant of Abraham too and you share in his brand.

Abraham's birth name was Abram. Its meaning is "noble father." After his birth, Abram lived a somewhat narrow, family-centered life under his father's leadership and in his family's home. As you read in a previous chapter, Abram married Sarai (whose name later changed to Sarah), and moved his family to Canaan where God placed a specific call on Abram's life. He told Abram he would be the father of many nations whose number would be greater than all the stars in the sky.

In sealing this covenant with Abram, God changed his name to Abraham, which means "the father of many nations." God promised to bless the whole world through Abraham. He is therefore not only the physical father of many nations but also the spiritual father of many nations. God essentially branded Abram as the father of many nations the moment He changed his name to Abraham. This demonstrates the branding and destiny-making power of a name.

When you were born you were given an individual name and you take on your family's name as well. When you come into a relationship with God, you are forever branded as a child and member of his family. I guess you could say you inherit at birth an "earthly" family brand but thanks to Abraham, when you are reborn by faith you inherit a "Heavenly" family brand.

THERE IS POWER IN A NAME

I have some members in my family who worked as cattlemen. I think it is interesting the importance they place on branding their herds. When a cattleman brands a cow, he is putting a sign on the animal that says this cow is a part of his herd; he is declaring that it belongs to him. But some cattlemen will choose not to brand their cows.

One reason is that should the cow get out of the fence and wander onto a road causing an accident, the cattleman does not want its ownership tied back to him. Cows do not have natural identifiable markings, making it difficult to connect it to a specific herd without the presence of a brand. If the cow carries a cattleman's brand, then the cattleman is responsible for the actions of the cow.

On the positive side, some beef cattle carrying a brand that represents a specific herd bring more money when they are sold at auction. The buyers recognize their brand as coming from a reputable herd known for producing quality beef. They know the cattle tend to be well cared for and fed high protein feed. Therefore the buyer is willing to pay a premium price for this cow because they recognize its brand value. Brands have power—both positive and negative.

Abraham was a man who walked with character and integrity. His defined value system was established on the promises of God. The tree representing his family was deeply rooted in faith. If you are a believer, your tree sprouts from Abraham's. You came through his generational lineage. Through faith, your family tree grows in the Orchard of God rooted from the tree of Abraham. You were created by God and given His spiritual DNA. You also carry Abraham's generational DNA. This makes you and your family a powerhouse of promise!

BUILDING YOUR BRAND

As a leader, you are called to make a difference in the lives of your family, friends, circles of influence, and the community in which you live. In order to make a positive difference, you must have the character and integrity that define a person of positive influence. What does this look like to you? How do you want your family to be perceived in the minds of others? These things are a part of your brand.

Our name is the imprint of our brand; however, our choices put meaning behind the imprint. You may have heard the saying, "a noun (brand) comes to life when accompanied by a verb (action)." The actions of your family create snapshots in the minds of others revealing what you stand for, your values, the traits making up your character, and the level of your integrity. Your brand doesn't have anything to do with the amount of money in your bank account, the person who designed your shoes, the neighborhood in which you live, the car you drive, or your social class.

Your family brand is established by who you are on the inside not how you appear on the outside.

You leave an imprint on the life of every single person with whom you come into contact. What does your imprint look like? Do you speak words of encouragement and affirmation into the lives of others? Are you willing to step outside of your comfort zone to meet the needs of others? Does your family support a specific organization by giving time, talents, and resources? Are you a person of positive influence in the lives of your family as well as those around you? Do you live a life others want to mirror? With every family decision you make you are establishing the meaning behind your brand.

PROTECTING YOUR BRAND

Every smart corporation out there understands the importance that brand identity plays in securing a strong position in the marketplace as well as its importance in determining overall success. Creating a brand that carries a strong message is the goal of every company. Their brand represents what they stand for in the minds of their consumers. Corporations work hard to establish and build strong brand identities so competitors don't steal their customers or shareholders.

Your family too must be on guard at all times. There are competitors out there trying to woo your shareholders—your family—away. Movies, video games, adult websites, television commercials, too many activities, the company you work for, all compete to steal away your family's time for one another. These distractions ultimately disconnect your hearts. When this happens, unhealthy things cloud your family's mirror making it difficult to see a clear reflection of the things that matter most in life.

These negative influences will compete for your time and attention from every possible angle. Your home should represent a safe haven, a lighthouse for your family. This is why establishing a family brand is so important. It protects what we hold out as important and establishes boundaries in which to live. It is important as a family to establish a brand that includes positive messaging to guard your hearts from the competitors working overtime to steal your unity and keep you from accomplishing your calling and purpose. Brand messaging is important because it helps to establish a positive sense of "family" image, encourages the family to dream together, and to believe in a strong collective future.

In advertising, repetition is the key to success. As an enterprise owner, you must communicate to your employees, "This is what we stand for." In order for the employees to stand behind the values of the company, they have to understand what values the company holds. In the same way, positioning and strengthening your family brand is about more than just jotting down a few happy phrases on a piece of paper and asking your family to uphold their message. It is strategically thinking about what you believe in and the influence you want to have in the lives you touch. It takes knowing the heart of each member of your family, recognizing their strengths, and then purposefully incorporating these into your actions.

Your Family Brand encompasses who your family is, what you stand for, and how you want to be known by others. It all comes down to where your heart is and who you serve.

With competition for your family's time and attention on the rise, making your home a safe haven where your family finds peace, strength, and inspiration is more important than ever. Establish a brand with your family that says we stand for something big and we will not lose our focus to things that have no lasting value.

REINVENTING YOUR BRAND

Is it possible to redefine your family brand? I believe it is. Corporate brands are redesigned and redefined all the time. They're changed for the purpose of making a greater impact and influence in their identified marketplace. Families can do the same.

Just like corporations, families can sometimes have a branch (individual) that isn't performing according to the company's standards and values. Even the healthiest tree can occasionally produce a bad apple. However, as the song goes, "One bad apple don't have to spoil the whole bunch."

People can't destroy your reputation unless you let them. It is possible to move your family in a different and more positive direction. Just as Abraham reached a point in his life where it was time to move on and become the leader for his family, you have the same opportunity in your family. Abraham led his family from Haran into Canaan. Abraham made the choice to obey God's call on *his* life, and in so doing he received blessing from God, as did every generation thereafter. He built a legacy of faith, honor, integrity, respect, and blessing. Not only did he prosper, but God multiplied his blessing beyond what the human mind can comprehend.

How did Abraham redirect the course and bring blessing over his family? Think back to Abraham's lineage. There were some great apples and some bad apples hanging from his family tree. Abraham chose to walk out unwavering faith in God. Remember his nephew Lot? Lot made different choices along his journey, and he ended up settling for less than God's best.

Abraham lived God's purposes on earth. He entrusted his life and his family to God's hands. He refused to settle for less by not living to the world's standards. He chose instead to view the world's rules and standards as the minimum, reaching instead toward Heaven's principles and values as the optimum. Abraham sought God's wisdom in every family matter. Through his action and faith-driven leadership he designed and defined a brand that stands unchanged today.

The seeds of Abraham continue to produce deeply rooted trees full of incredible fruit. When you choose to walk in faith, your family tree will sprout from the well-established trees growing in Abraham's spiritual orchard. Nourished well, great fruit will grow and blessings will flow.

STAND BY YOUR BRAND

Your family brand helps you to not only identify what is important to you as a family but to filter your activities and life through these values and principles as well. Your family brand builds a greater sense of unity and encourages outward rather than inward focus. Hopefully, like me, you want your kids to have a continuing desire to stay connected to your family. Establishing your own unique family brand gives you a sense of family identity and encourages family unity and loyalty. Once you establish the things you stand for you are then able to establish a family brand you can stand behind.

RECAP:

1. Your name has an instantaneous emotion tied to it, good or bad. What do you want others to feel when they hear your family name?
2. You carry God's brand through Abraham, which then blends with the brand you are creating for your own family name.
3. As you make decisions and choices for you and your family in business and in life, make sure you are filtering those decisions through your family brand so you can be sure your choices support the life and the future you want your family to have.

CHAPTER SEVEN

MY WAY

"Many persons have a wrong idea of what constitutes true
happiness. It is not attained through self-gratification but
through fidelity to a worthy PURPOSE."
— Helen Keller, *The Miracle Worker*, my emphasis

THE DOOR SHUT with a bang as the young man exited the factory. It was
the twenty-first building he had entered while seeking employment.
The grip of the falling economy had squeezed the life from many families,
including his. And his job search had gone on for weeks. Tall and willowy
in stature, he was just sixteen and the youngest of five children. Six months
before, his father passed away. His mom was working two jobs trying to
make ends meet. He needed a job to help provide food for his family.

The sun was setting and darkness would soon fall, so he decided to take
a short-cut home. He turned down a poorly lit side street. The shadows
deepened as he neared the end of the street. Out of nowhere a bright
yellow light appeared from the second building on the right.

He approached and peered into the window. There, leaning over a machine was an old man piecing together a man's jacket with thread. He walked to the slightly opened doorway, and entered the room. He smiled shyly, extended his hand and said, "My name is Jack and I am looking for employment. My mom needs help caring for my family. Would you happen to be in need of an extra set of hands to help you make more beautiful clothes?"

The old man raised his head and looked Jack over from head to toe as he slowly stood from the machine. It felt like twenty minutes to Jack, but eventually the old man reached out his hand and said, "To someone who recognizes my work as beautiful, I am willing to give a chance."

Jack was filled with energy and excitement as they shook hands. He went to work that very next day. The old man started by teaching Jack how quality clothes begin with a vision. Once the proper material is added the result is a masterpiece of superior craftsmanship. The store always seemed full of energy and excitement as all the best people desired to wear the fine clothing from the local tailor. Jack soaked up all the knowledge the old man offered as he willingly performed any duty he was asked to complete.

Over time Jack's skill and knowledge increased. As he learned the craft, he eventually earned the title of tailor. Soon the master tailor taught him how to go to the market and select the best material. The old man continued to mentor Jack, teaching him how to manage his money well and pay all the vendors at market.

Ten years passed quickly. One day Jack looked around and realized it was he who was doing the majority of the work in the tailor shop. Soon after this realization, the old man approached Jack and said, "You have been a faithful servant and I have taught you all I know about making quality clothing. My eyes are old and the time has come for me to rest. So, I want you to take over this business."

Tears came to Jack's eyes as he realized the dream of owning his own shop was finally coming true. They negotiated the terms and he gladly agreed to pay the old man, realizing if he had not had faith in and mentored

Jack, Jack would never have achieved his current level of success. The days grew longer, but he now worked with a new intensity and energy knowing he was growing his company.

Jack married his high school sweetheart, Ellen. The days flew as he felt like the luckiest man alive. She helped in the store as their reputation for making quality clothing spread far and wide. Jack learned from the old man to purchase only the finest material as he traveled to the far regions of the west to secure the best of the best. With time, he became a shrewd negotiator. By negotiating better purchase prices and managing his inventory, Jack quickly achieved greater cash flow making it possible to open additional locations.

At the same time his business was growing his family increased in size to three with the birth of their son. He and Ellen also added numerous tailors and sales assistants to manage the other locations. Before long, their company was the largest of its kind. The family was known in most influential circles as being successful, wealthy, and honest. The company's reputation thrived.

The years went by quickly, and suddenly one day Jack looked into the mirror and realized he was now an old man! His eyesight was deteriorating, as was his desire to work long hours and go numerous days without rest. He talked with Ellen and decided the time had arrived for them to transfer the company to their son.

The son, however, had no interest in his dad's company. But he was addicted to the lifestyle the company had allowed him to enjoy. He worked in the tailor shop as a young boy, but soon playing with his friends became more important. He left tasks undone to pursue more fun activities. Observing this, his father would sigh and hope that his son would grow to love the job as he had himself when he was young. Sadly, his son never did.

As Jack and Ellen decided to visit with their son about transitioning the company, they were met with anxiety as they did not know how it would turn out.

He began the conversation by reminding his son of how he had come to own the business—how the old man had poured his heart into him, providing the wisdom and direction. He recounted his and Ellen's years of sacrifice and sweat that made their current level of success possible. The son listened intently as his heart pounded with excitement realizing the company would finally be his. He was eager to make changes and increase the success of the company.

Jack spoke softly as he said to his son, "We have decided to either sell you the company at an agreed-upon value, or freely give you all the knowledge and wisdom that the old man gave me, so you can start and grow your own company from scratch."

Jack took Ellen's hand and said, "Son, which one of these options has the greatest value for you?"

ENTITLEMENT

The story of Jack the tailor contains elements I have personally witnessed in families numerous times in my career. The parents of successful companies employed a strong work ethic, high reputation, and a good moral compass. They lived within their means as they have planned toward retirement. The children who stand to inherit the company, just like Jack's son, are born into a world where their parents have already achieved some success and tended to shower their children with privileges, rather than instilling the same values they had.

Most of the time, the parents' motives are pure, but these tendencies usually have a major negative impact on the kids. They are often enslaved by what is called an entitlement mentality.

So, how did Jack's son respond to his parents' offer? Well, to finish the story, he accepted the company—believing he was smarter than his dad and could take it to greater levels of success. Did he achieve such a level? Sadly he did not. Why? Because he held the world's twisted definition of what defines "value."

I can identify with the parable of Jack the tailor because the son's sense of direction was just like mine at one time. His first thought was, "What can I get?" not "What can I give?" Why did he think this way? It's possible he was holding on to some deep resentment. Perhaps he felt his dad's company took his father away too much. And maybe this resentment led to an entitlement mindset.

Entitlement means "believing you have a right to something." We sometimes feel entitled to something because we think once we get that something, we will feel better about something else we didn't get and thought we deserved. It's compensation. For example, Jack may have felt that by inheriting his dad's company it would fill the space of abandonment he felt when his dad showed up for the company but didn't show up in his life. Generational planning requires making choices now that will affect the future. It goes far beyond just the tangible. However, can the tangible and intangible coexist?

Yes! I believe it is possible to build monetary wealth and wealth of character at the same time. To accomplish this, however, a family must deal with the issues of entitlement and giftedness when it comes to determining who will inherit the family assets.

HISTORICAL MINDSETS

Over the past century, generational differences have become more evident as we see definite trends emerging among each new generation. Demographers have identified four primary groups among the people born in the 20th century. The first group is the Traditionalists—born between 1900 and 1945. This group experienced three wars, the Great Depression, the New Deal, the rise of multinational corporations and the emergence of the Space Age. During the time period in which they grew up, they experienced hard times followed by times of prosperity.

Those who lived through the Great Depression found it a transforming experience. The lack and widespread economic hardship left a deep mark on that generation, producing a cautious, frugal mentality which carried over and into the workplace. This generation moved from the farms into the factories and relished the opportunity to prove a strong work ethic, faithfulness to the company, and a belief that authority is based on seniority and tenure.

Next in the generational line are the Baby Boomers, who have birth years from 1946 to 1964. Personally, I am a Baby Boomer, with a birth year of 1959. We experienced the civil rights movement, the Vietnam War, the assassinations of President Kennedy and Martin Luther King Jr., the sexual revolution, and the Cold War. We were promised "The American Dream," and all we had to do to achieve it was set our sights on a goal and it would be ours. We experienced the birth of major electronic media during our formative years with the introduction of television. Soon a TV was a central fixture in every household in the country.

I personally believe the introduction of television is where the seeds of the entitlement mentality were planted. Television commercials in the 1960s and 1970s created a type of "White Picket Fence" syndrome encouraging people to believe that everything could be theirs and with a minimal price to pay. This produced a generation of workaholics, highly driven and competitive individuals who challenged authority and birthed numerous entrepreneurial businesses eventually changing the landscape of American business.

During the the 70s, the model of the family began to change as moms entered the work force to help better accomplish the "American Dream." Just as in the case of Jack the Tailor, families began showering the fruits of their labor upon their children to minimize the guilt of time spent away from them. Parents desired to minimize their children's exposure to the difficult times of life they had encountered during their own childhoods.

The next generation to come along were the Baby Busters—individuals born between 1965 and 1983. This group experienced Watergate, the energy crisis, dual-income families, the end of the Cold War, and the explosion of single-parenting. They are also known as the first generation who will not do as well financially as their parents. Their perceptions have been shaped by growing up and having to take care of themselves while watching politicians lie, parents lose their jobs, and families ripped apart by divorce.

They are suspicious of Boomer values, are highly educated, unimpressed with authority, have a high degree of brand loyalty, but have a totally different work ethic than that of prior generations. Busters are also known as the first "day care" generation since most grew up in two-parent working homes.

The Mosaics make up the most recent generation. These are individuals born between the years 1984 and 2002. They have experienced the explosive growth of technology like no other generation before them. They have also experienced the negativity advanced technology ushered in with it—school shootings, terrorist attacks (including September 11, 2001), and medical crises. A large percentage of children from this generation are children of divorce, increasing the number of blended families. The world is literally at their fingertips as the world has become mobile through the use of cell phones.

Yes, they are known as coddled kids by their parents and are also the first generation of children with most every moment of their days scheduled with some type of activity. Their view of the world is different than every other generation before them. For example, their lifestyles are more diverse, including education, career, family, values, and leisure. They don't want to be defined by "normal." They are marrying and starting families much later in life.

According to a report in 2012 by the Barna Group, a three-year study of the latter two generations revealed:

There are a few things both Busters and Mosaics share in common. They share the fact that relationships are the driving force in their lives. Being loyal to friends is one of their highest values. They have a strong need to belong usually to a tribe or other loyal people who know them well and appreciate them. But they also desire fierce individualism. They tend to be more skeptical of leaders, products, and institutions. (Busters tend to express skepticism layered with cynicism, and Mosaics do so with extreme self-confidence.) They do not trust things that seem too perfect, accepting that life comes with its share of messiness and off-the-wall experiences and people. Mosaics are influenced more than all the other generations by the media. (*UnChristian* by David Kinnaman and Gabe Lyons.)

Unfortunately, the entitlement mindset many Busters and Mosaics carry today has been handed down from the previous generation. Their parents have sheltered them more than any other past generation—hoping to protect them from hardship and the evils of the world.

My experience has shown that, until a family identifies the false belief patterns within its family's unit, it will be difficult to accomplish the call to succeed that God has upon the family. Establishing what I call a Generational Family Plan is almost impossible.

Communication is the key to this process. I have been fortunate to work with families and help them identify the areas where their views may not align with God's Word concerning ownership, stewardship, and His call for all family members to have a positive impact on the world.

RENEWING OUR MINDS

Let's return to the story of Abraham and Lot. We have already seen that Lot was following Abraham when he left Egypt and the quarreling began among the herdsmen.

Abraham gave Lot first choice of the land and Lot chose the "greener grass." This story is ingrained in my mind because Abraham displayed a "traditionalist" mindset. This mindset has impressed countless generations of Bible readers because it demonstrates an unselfish commitment to family and respect for God's ability to reward the unselfish.

As we know, Lot jumped at the opportunity to choose first. It was the "me-centered" approach. Of course, Lot had received many benefits from his association with Abraham (his mentor). So we shouldn't be too surprised to see the younger man behaving like a member of the Buster or Mosaic generation. Lot viewed himself as *deserving* of the best and choicest.

The fruits of Abraham's honorable life had spilled over to Lot, increasing the size of his flocks, herds, and tents. By taking the seemingly easier, me-centered route, Lot landed smack-dab in the middle of Sodom and Gomorrah. There he experienced total devastation in the years to come.

We also see an entitlement mindset displayed in the life of Isaac's children, Jacob and Esau. As you may know, Jacob deceived his brother Esau and received his father's blessing under false pretenses. Not only did the family blessing bring tremendous emotional validation, it also entitled the firstborn to a majority of the family assets. Yes, Esau had sold his birthright to his brother for a bowl of stew, but Jacob clearly deceived Esau when he stole the blessing.

As a child of God we are rightful heirs to the God-given heritage promised us through Abraham. Through this heritage we have certain rights. We also have rights to certain things by virtue of being a part of our family tree. However, we must receive both of these through faith and the heart of stewardship to fully appreciate these blessings.

In order to have that proper mindset, we must be intentional about what we choose to dwell on and the thoughts that enter our minds. I believe this is why, Scripturally, we are instructed to renew our minds—so we can be transformed instead of conformed to the world's twisted standards.

Do not conform any longer to the pattern of this world, but be transformed by the renewing of your mind. Then you will be able to test and approve what God's will is—his good, pleasing and perfect will. –Romans 12:2 NIV

DON'T DELAY

For nine years I enjoyed a special friendship with Jim. Our relationship on earth ended on a winter night in the late 1990s. Jim was seventy-two years old when he suffered a catastrophic brain aneurism. In the preceding months we had numerous discussions about his son, Drake. Jim undoubtedly had the right skill set and experience to manage well on an ongoing basis the company he and Evelyn had built. But Jim was starting to recognize that his son had an entitlement mindset and did not possess the giftedness needed to successfully manage the company.

Eventually, Jim decided it was time to discuss his concerns with Evelyn and his daughter. He felt Drake needed to exit the company and he needed to put together a transitional plan. It was important for Jim to ensure a smooth transition corporately, yet keep Drake's self-worth and preserve family unity. For a reason only God knows, that conversation never happened. Jim left this world before his planned family meeting. The opportunity to put his company on a solid footing for the future passed with his death.

After Jim's funeral, Drake purchased his mother's share of the company. This freed Evelyn from being financially tied to the company that now belonged to her son. She was able to receive outright the assets she needed to provide for herself during the remainder of her lifetime.

Over the last several years, the fears Jim and I had about the company have been validated. Drake would not accept any professional advice from his dad's circle of influence. He continued with "me-approach" goals that included a private school for his children, a larger home, new vehicles, and a lifestyle lived way beyond his means. Because of these poor choices, the company is in bankruptcy with a slim chance of returning to the vibrant company Jim built.

Looking back, I often wonder what Jim should have done differently. Remember, he did understand his call and giftedness as God blessed his life. As with most parents, it was hard for Jim to accept that God created his child with skill-sets, talents, and abilities very different from his own. No matter how much coaching or mentoring Drake received, he was naturally going to struggle to find contentment and success at the helm of the company his dad desperately wanted him to carry forward. Add Drake's entitlement mentality to that equation and you'll understand why disaster was the inevitable outcome for Drake and for the company his father had worked so hard and long to build.

I also believe Jim's mistake was waiting too long to make the hard decisions he needed to regarding managing his current assets and future-oriented planning. He did not consider the possibility that tomorrow might not come. While you shouldn't live solely *for* tomorrow, you do need to live *mindful* of tomorrow. The decisions of today will affect the outcome of tomorrow.

Since Jim's death, I have come to understand that the legacy most leaders think they need to pass forward is about what they *do* rather than who they *are*. In other words, they believe that the company they've built is what needs to be transferred to their heirs, (regardless of whether they're gifted or called to successfully run it) rather than selling it to an outside party and simply transferring the purchase price to their kids. If God designed a child to be in ministry, a florist, a writer, or a teacher, would it not be more beneficial to help facilitate those gifts for the family into the next generation? Wouldn't that represent a legacy of high positive impact?

ENGAGING YOUR HEIRS

Helping the next generation to be fully engaged in their truest, highest calling is vital to fulfilling your family legacy. This can be accomplished through the following simple actions: understanding, communicating, and releasing.

Understanding

I believe most individuals do not really understand their core gifts and talents. A wise family leader will seek to understand his children's differences and gifts. He'll also encourage his children to identify their unique gifts and strengths through the various analysis and tests that are now available. I have found these tools extremely helpful in working with numerous clients and their families.

Communicating

Acquiring information and being able to communicate it is also vital to the long-term success of your family. Spend some time listening and communicating together. Talk about the practices, attributes, and values that make your family unique. How do you want to be known collectively to others in your circle of influence? What should the "brand" of your name represent?

Take an inventory of each heart. I encourage you to do a SOAR (strengths, opportunities, aspirations, and results) analysis. This will help you to not only identify your natural strengths and abilities but also empower you with information to help your family reach its greatest level of success.

It is important for you to manage your communication with your family—extended and immediate—well. Take time to listen and hear from each member of the family and validate his or her contributions to the process. This will bring blessings rather than burdens.

Releasing

As parents go through this process, they must come to understand two points. The first is that it's okay to have differences of opinion as long as both parties honor and respect each other in the communication process. The second is to decipher and understand your children's giftedness and encourage them in their gifts even if it isn't what you personally envisioned for your child.

Good children are frequently caught between a desire to please and honor their parents and what they know is the true calling in their lives. Releasing your children from your expectations, and allowing them to live according to God's expectations is the greatest blessing you can give them. By allowing them to expand their own gifts, they will have great impact as they accept and live out their calling "guilt free."

ESTABLISHING AN ABRAHAMIC LEGACY

Abraham's life reveals that attaining spiritual maturity is a lifelong process. Spiritual leaders don't take shortcuts. Abraham was one hundred years old when Isaac was born. He waited twenty-five years for God to carry out His promise. Abraham learned a lesson about the difference between God's timing and human timing. God sees things from an eternal perspective. People see things from a temporal view.

Spiritual leaders invite disaster when they panic and assume they must take matters into their own hands. When spiritual leaders wait patiently on the Lord, regardless of how long it takes, God always proves Himself absolutely true to His Word. Sometimes the time it takes God's promise to be realized can seem eternally long. But a promise fulfilled by God is always worth the wait. Many family leaders would see major accomplishments and breakthroughs in the lives of their children if only they were willing to wait as long as necessary to see God accomplish "His will."

When you are obedient to God's call in the lives of your family, you experience God working through your life and come to know more about God's character. Abraham was an obedient family leader. Abraham understood his actions did not affect him alone, but that his obedience to God would impact generations to follow.

Abraham was a Godly man and a Godly leader of his family. He became the patriarch of a nation; he became a father of the faithful. Abraham was also far from perfect; he made many mistakes. Yet his heart was open before God, and God chose to develop him into a man of faith.

God didn't choose Abraham because of his leadership ability. He chose Abraham because of his heart of obedience and faith. The key to Abraham's success as a patriarch was that he came to know God and he allowed God to transform him into a strong family leader. When you strive to have your heart right before God, then in return, God promises to show Himself strong and bless your family lineage for many generations to come. And that is the definition of living well and leaving a lasting legacy!

RECAP

1. Be fully aware of the entitlement mindset instilled by the world and mindfully guard your heart and your legacy from that mindset in both you and your heirs.
2. Help your children discover their own unique giftedness and release them from your own expectations while guiding them to the great things God has for them instead.
3. Allow God to transform you into a strong family leader, just as He did for Abraham.

CHAPTER EIGHT

RECEIVING YOUR BLESSING

"The family blessing not only provides people a much-needed sense of personal acceptance, it also plays an important part in protecting and even freeing them to develop intimate relationships ... The best defense against a child's longing for imaginary acceptance is to provide him or her with genuine acceptance."
— John Trent and Gary Smalley, *The Blessing*

EVERY DAY IS A GIFT—full of opportunities to speak words of affirmation and blessing into the lives of the people you love. When you speak words of blessing over someone, you are releasing God's power and favor to work in and through their lives.

Our world tends to put the highest value on things—status, money, stuff, and more stuff. The truth is God values people above all temporal things. The people God places in your life are important to Him and therefore should be important to you, too. One of the greatest gifts you can give your spouse, your children, your family, and those in your circle

of influence, is a word of affirmation or blessing. A word of encouragement, affirmation, and blessing spoken at a timely moment can change
everything for that person. Words are powerful. We must choose them
wisely and speak them with wisdom and love.

This chapter is probably the most important chapter in this book
to me. I understand personally, as I will share later, the importance of
speaking such words.

Let me tell you the story about a woman named Rebekah and her
husband Isaac. They had twin sons, Esau and Jacob. Esau was an out-
doorsman who loved to hunt and hang out in the fields while Jacob, his
younger brother, was quiet and stayed near the house. Isaac preferred
his firstborn son Esau, while Jacob—born just minutes later, but second
in line as an heir—was his mother's favorite.

When Isaac was an old man, he asked Esau to go hunting and prepare a
meal for him before he died. Isaac wanted to give his oldest son his blessing
before he died. Rebekah was standing nearby and overheard Isaac talking
to Esau. She wanted Jacob to have Isaac's blessing, so she instructed Jacob
to bring her two young goats so that she could prepare a meal.

Since Isaac's eyes were weak and he could not see well, Rebekah schemed
and came up with a plan to trick Isaac into thinking that Jacob was his
other son, Esau. Rebekah put Esau's best clothes on Jacob and covered
his hands and neck with the goat skins so that Jacob's smooth skin would
feel more like Esau's hairy arms.

Rebekah prepared the tasty meal and sent Jacob in with it in order to
deceive his father. When Isaac asked, "Who are you?" Jacob lied and said
he was Esau and he was bringing the meat of the animal he had hunted.
When the father asked how he had killed the animal so quickly, Jacob
lied again and said God had helped him. Isaac asked Jacob to come closer
so he could touch him and make sure he was Esau. When Isaac touched
Jacob he said, "Your voice sounds like Jacob's, but your hands are hairy
like Esau." He asked if this was really Esau. Jacob lied yet again and said,
"Yes, I am." So Isaac gave his blessing to Jacob. (Read Genesis 27.)

Just as Jacob was leaving, Esau returned. He brought the food his father had requested and asked for the blessing. Then Isaac began to tremble, realizing he had been tricked by the lies of Jacob. He gave his younger son the power to be master over his older son. Esau cried and begged for a blessing from his father. The best Isaac could do was promise that one day Esau would be free from Jacob's power.

Why do you suppose Esau cried at the loss of the blessing that was rightfully his? Do you think he was disappointed at discovering he had lost his inheritance? I don't think that was it at all. During this time, the oldest son's inheritance was part of his birthright and gave him a double share in his father's wealth. The truth is Esau had already sold his birthright to his brother Jacob earlier for a pot of red stew.

Esau was not grieved because of the "things" he'd lost. He was devastated because he lost the blessing of his father—something very personal and very important. In the Old Testament era, once a blessing was spoken it was irreversible and irrevocable. Isaac could never transfer that blessing to Esau. There was no "undo" button. It was too late. Esau was so grieved he asked his father a second time to bless him. But Isaac could not give Esau a blessing; it had been taken by Jacob. Esau would never hear the words of affirmation and acceptance he so longed to hear spoken from his father's mouth.

WHY BLESSING MATTERS

God created us for fellowship. Every human being craves acceptance. In every place and in every time, people simply want to know they matter to someone. We all long for acceptance and affirmation—from the moment we are born. This is the foundation on which every authentic and satisfying relationship with God begins.

Receiving a spoken blessing enables you to move forward in life with confidence and purpose. In the absence of blessing, many individuals flounder through life never really understanding why they are here because they don't perceive their true worth and value.

I JUST WANT TO BE ENOUGH

As the youngest of five children I had a unique vantage point for watching our family culture and the influence it had in the daily lives of my four siblings. I already shared how my parents provided teachings of faith, integrity, strong work ethic, and a strong family community in our home.

They were both hardworking people who wanted their children to have great experiences in life. They took us on family camping trips every year to see sights all across the United States. Family was important to my parents.

I know my parents both loved me and showed it in numerous ways. But they never really affirmed or blessed me in the way I needed. Do I hold a grudge or blame them? Of course not. They parented me in the way they had learned from their parents and in accordance with the light they had at that time.

Not until I read the book *The Blessing* by John Trent and Gary Smalley did I begin to realize what was missing in my soul. What was lacking in my life, and what I so desired was a spoken blessing and words of affirmation. I ultimately realized that, just as God blessed Abraham with a bright future, numerous offspring, a specific community, and a place to call home, God offers me this same blessing. That was wonderful news!

As we learned in a previous chapter, the Abrahamic covenant is ours to receive if, by faith, we choose to accept God's blessing. This truth has allowed me to receive something ever more powerful—a blessing my parents did not know how to give, but that I desperately desired and needed.

I have also come to understand that just as it is impossible to teach what you don't know, it is impossible to give something you don't understand. My parents did not speak blessing and affirmation into my life because they did not understand completely what it meant to do so, nor did they understand the importance in doing so. And for my part, I didn't realize blessing was what I was missing until later in my adult life, so I never asked to receive it.

Just as you cannot give something you don't have to give, neither can you pass forward a Christian heritage to the next generation if you have not come into a relationship with God. You must first receive through faith this free gift from God before it can become a part of your legacy.

FIVE ELEMENTS OF THE BLESSING

In their book, *The Blessing*,[1] authors Gary Smalley and John Trent describe the blessing as having five main elements:

1. A meaningful and appropriate touch.
2. A spoken message.
3. Attaching a high value to the one being blessed.
4. Picturing a special future to fulfill the blessing.
5. An active commitment to fulfill the blessing.

Let's take a glance at each one of these five elements in order to understand their importance in extending the family blessing.

TOUCH: THE FELT BLESSING

Throughout the Bible there are examples of blessings given—and each time touch plays a role in the process. Placing a kiss on the cheek, offering a hug, and the laying on of hands, are all examples of blessing extended through touch.

Meaningful and appropriate touch has many benefits. It communicates warmth, kindness, acceptance, and affirmation and lends itself to physical

[1] John Trent and Gary Smalley, *The Blessing*, 1993 and 2011, (Thomas Nelson Inc. Nashville, Tennessee.)

health. Should you wish to bless someone special in your life, whether a family member or friend, let the power of touch play a role in bestowing your blessing.

SPOKEN WORD

One of the most basic ways to extend "the blessing" is to put it into actual words. Author Gary Chapman, in his book *The Five Love Languages*,[2] calls this using the language of "words of affirmation." He says:

> Words of affirmation, your spoken praise and appreciation, will fall like rain on parched soil. Before long you will see new life sprouting in your marriage, relationships with your children, or others as they respond to your words of love. (*The Five Love Languages*, Gary Chapman)

As we saw in the example of Esau and Jacob mentioned earlier in the chapter, Isaac "spoke" a blessing to Jacob. It is significant that God says, *In the beginning was the Word, the Word was with God, and the Word was God* (John 1:1 NIV). This Scripture illustrates the importance God placed on words. He is the Word. There is nothing more beautiful than to see a blessing spoken into the heart of someone blossom into a beautiful flower, nourished by faith and fortified through grace.

VALUING THE ONE BEING BLESSED

To effectively communicate a blessing, the words (spoken or written) must attribute high value to the person being blessed. You may have

---

[2] Chapman, Gary D., *The Five Love Languages: the Secret to Love That Lasts.* (Chicago, IL: Northfield Pub., 2010. Print)

heard the phrase, "painting a word-picture." This is true when you are speaking value into someone's life. You really can paint a picture with words. Use your words to paint a picture of whom your family members are in Christ. Valuing another person releases him or her to pursue God's blessing for his or her life. It leads to wholeness in Christ.

Ask God to show you the attributes and strengths He has placed in the hearts of your spouse, children, family members, and others in your life. When He reveals their gifts and talents, call those talents out through words of affirmation and blessing. Speak God's truth into the lives of those He places directly and indirectly in your path.

THE FUTURE IS BRIGHT

By naming and articulating the gifts, strengths, and abilities God has given someone, we speak blessing over their future. God speaks often in His Word about the future He has waiting for us in Heaven. For example, He says "Then I saw a new heaven and a new earth ... I saw the Holy City, the new Jerusalem, coming down out of heaven from God." (Revelation 21:1a-2a NIV)

We need to visualize a bright future for our children and spouses and speak these blessings into their lives. There is something transforming about focusing our thoughts on eternity. Thoughts usher in actions. The Bible tells us, "For as he thinks in his heart, so is he." (Proverbs 23:7a NKJV) Thoughts are very powerful. By speaking truth and blessing into the lives of others we are empowering them to think upward as they live outward.

God has no limitations; once you are in Christ, you don't either. Encourage the people God has purposefully placed in your life to focus beyond the finish line—that's where the real prize is.

ACTIVE COMMITMENT

It is vital that a patriarch or matriarch of a family stand behind any spoken blessings he or she gave. It is important to seek the direction of the Holy Spirit in confirming the spoken blessing over others. Active Commitment means putting action behind your words of blessing. What you say is empty if what you do does not back it up. Spend quality time listening and engaging in your spouse's, children's, family's, and friends' lives. The one thing you can never get back is lost time. Make the moments count. Affirm the blessing you've spoken by empowering and influencing them through the way you walk out your daily life.

THE POWER OF THE BLESSING

Empowering spoken blessing is God's way of imparting His image and vision into the soul of a person. That's why extending a blessing over those you care about actually causes their souls to prosper. And according to the Bible, soul prosperity results in health and abundance in all areas of life. (See 3 John 1:2) When you bless someone, you kneel before them in humility and literally empower that person to flourish and prosper in life. I don't believe that prosperity refers only to finances. True prosperity affects all areas of a person's life. For example, when you bless your children, you empower them to prosper in every area of their lives; spiritually, physically, emotionally, financially, in their marriages, over their children, in their careers, and through their ministries.

THE GREATEST BLESSING

The Son of God spoke the greatest possible blessing over your life through three spoken words: "It is finished!" Through His death on the cross and resurrection three days later, He blessed you with opportunity to receive eternal life. You are enough! God says you are His prized possession. You are worthy by His grace. He calls you His very own. The moment you give your life to Him, you receive the Father's blessing! Your past is now irrelevant. You may have never received the blessing of your earthly father. That's unfortunate, but that no longer matters. You can find redemption and restoration in knowing you have the blessing of your Heavenly Father, who loves you just as you are and right where you are.

You can move forward today in the knowledge that you are more than enough. The future is bright and full of possibility.

WHEN THE BLESSING DOESN'T COME

Like me, maybe you've never received an earthly parent's spoken blessing. You may have spent untold time and energy struggling to find a sense of worthiness or to prove your worthiness to others. It is important to get this truth deeply imbedded in your soul: People do NOT and CANNOT define your worth or determine your value.

At the same time, extending blessing is our call as believers in God and as the leaders in our families. Still, I also know it doesn't always happen. That's why it's important to know that when you come into a relationship with God, you receive His blessing immediately—a blessing that is irreversible and irrevocable. You are God's child by choice and He declares you more than enough ... period. No earthly blessing? That is okay—you have His Heavenly blessing.

WHAT EXACTLY IS MY INHERITED BLESSING?

Let's look at the blessing God spoke (paraphrased) over Abraham and a blessing He speaks over you and me still today (see Genesis 12:1-7).

"I will show you a land and give it to you."
(God will reveal your spiritual destiny.)

"I will make you a great nation."
(God will make your spiritual descendants great.)

"I will bless you."
(God will bless you.)

"I will make your name great."
(He will make your name great; it will represent character and integrity.)

"You will be a blessing."
(He will make you a blessing.)

"I will bless them who bless you."
(He will bless those who bless you.)

"I will come against those who come against you."
(He will serve as your defender and protector when attacked.)

"In Me all families of the earth will be blessed."
(In Me your family for all generations forward will be blessed.)

"All the land which you see, to you I will give it forever."
(Everything God reveals to me is mine.)

"I will also give the land to your descendants forever."
(My blessings from God will extend to all future generations of believers.)

"Walk through the land, for I will give it to you."
(Wherever God leads me, that spiritual territory is mine.)

"I am your shield."
(God is my shield.)

"I am your great reward."
(God is my great reward.)

"He that is born of your own body will be your heir."
(I will bring forth spiritual heirs.)

"Your heirs will be as many as the stars in the sky."
(My spiritual heirs will be as many as the stars in the sky.)

"I am the Lord who brought you out of Ur of the Chaldees to give you this land to inherit."
(God brought me out of my past through His grace and into my spiritual inheritance.)

"I will make my covenant between Me and you (Abraham)."
(This is a supernatural covenant established between God and me.)

"Your name will be called Abraham rather than Abram."
(God will change my spiritual identity to reflect His call and purpose.)

"I will make you abundantly fruitful."
(I will bare much fruit in every area of my life.)

"I will make nations of you."
(I will multiply spiritually and empower the future for many generations.)

"My covenant blessing is everlasting."
(God's covenant blessing over me is everlasting.)

BLESSED TO BE A BLESSING

You have an incredible opportunity to be an example that will cause the world to desire to know God. I believe strongly in the importance of releasing generational blessings, legacies we pass forward to our children, our children's children, and the many generations that follow. Your legacy impacts not just your family, but the world around you. God has empowered you with everything you need to step up and make an impact in the lives of others. Remember spoken blessings create a ripple effect from generation to generation. You are blessed by God to pass forward a legacy of abundant blessing!

RECAP

1. Everyone desires affirmations and blessings from birth. Regardless of how old or young your children are, it is never too late to affirm them and bless them.
2. Incorporate the five elements of blessing into your family.
3. Regardless of whether your parents passed on blessings or affirmations to you, you have been given abundant blessings from your Heavenly Father. It is your right to receive them, embrace them, and pass them on.

CHAPTER NINE

FROM GENERATION TO GENERATION

*"Our heritage and ideals, our code and standards—the things
we live by and teach our children—are preserved or diminished
by how freely we exchange ideas and feelings." —Walt Disney*

I S YOUR FAMILY TREE DIFFERENT from everyone else's? You bet it is. I've worked alongside many families from all walks of life. But one thing I have come to realize over the years is the similarities that thread each family tree together. Every family has a heritage—a past that influences its current traditions and general direction. That's why every family needs to have a series of ongoing conversations about things like the blessing, entitlement mindsets, gifts and aptitudes, and the concept of stewardship.

Many have recognized that the family unit as a whole is broken in our culture. It is broken because there are no perfect people—and people make up families.

It is important to understand the consequences of refusing to own our individual brokenness and to work toward the healing of generational wounds. Instead of passing forward a God-given legacy, we will pass forward the same brokenness we inherited from past generations. Guilt, disappointment, fear, and a failure to discover our God-given call all work to keep us from pursuing God's best for our lives.

You must come to understand that God has called you to your family. And with that calling comes responsibility. As a leader, you must accept this call by faith and press forward to impact, not just the next generation, but generations to come. The Apostle Paul said it this way: *I press on toward the goal to win the prize for which God has called me heavenward in Christ Jesus* (Philippians 3:14 NIV).

Understanding your family heritage is important because it has an impact on what you believe, stand for, and have faith in. It also impacts the important values on which you stand individually as well as collectively as a family unit. Your family heritage plays a significant role in how you establish and live out your immediate family legacy. It also influences the strength of your family tree's roots.

I have created a five-step process we will explore together through the next five chapters that is titled, "Generation to Generation—Protecting Family Values.®" The purpose of this plan is to guide you through the steps necessary to define your family legacy. This process gives you the framework from which you will ultimately establish your family life plan. These five steps include: family heritage, vision, values, relationships, and assets.

This process is not about how much money your family is worth. No, it's about something far more important. It's about defining your legacy so the baton may be transferred effectively to the next generation. So let's roll up our sleeves and dive in.

FAMILY HERITAGE

First, let's explore why understanding your family heritage is important. My experience has shown that identifying your family lineage gives you a clearer picture of how the past influences the present. And with a new generation of web-based tools, a map of the multiple trees making up your family orchard can grow right before your very eyes at the push of a button.

It may not seem important for you to learn about your ancestors. Nevertheless, there may be some key information about the legacy you were handed hiding in the background information about your great-grandparents, grandparents, and parents—information that may be helpful to you in establishing some general family history.

I covered the generational differences from the last century's demographic groups in chapter seven. Now let's look at some of the views the generations before you held in regard to money, religion, work ethic, and values. As you think through some of their views on these subjects, identifying how they affected family relationships is important, as you will see both consistent positive and negative patterns.

In the previous chapters we examined how a family heritage can be compared to an apple orchard that grows different types of apple trees. The positive patterns you see within your family heritage represent the healthy extended-family trees in your orchard from which you continue to root and sprout stronger immediate-family trees.

The negative patterns represent the extended-family trees that must be pruned in order to ensure your immediate-family tree maintains its health as it sprouts, takes root, and begins to produce new fruit of its own.

Left alone, the unhealthy trees will become diseased and prevent others from producing healthy fruit. Pruning is necessary to keep each tree, and ultimately the family orchard, healthy. The following are two personal examples of pruning within my own family orchard. In 1991, I traveled to a small rural town in Texas to visit my grandparents' grave. As the youngest of five children, I knew my grandmother, but my grandfather passed away before I was born.

I had recently entered counseling to work through the aftermath of the collapse of a difficult ten-year marriage and the resulting painful divorce. I wanted to deal with the emotional scarring and negative thoughts that ran rampant through my mind. I believed I needed to begin grafting a stronger root system into my family tree in order for new growth to begin in my life.

I realized in order to move forward toward a better place in my personal life I needed to evaluate the relationships and influences from my past. As I stood over my grandparents' graves, I prayed that any generational sin, bondage, negative thoughts, emotional scarring, and depression would end with my generation.

I wish I could tell you that everything changed for me overnight. But, it didn't. It has been an ongoing process. Yet, by better understanding the influences of my past, owning the consequences of choices I consciously make in my present, and through seeking forgiveness and restoration from negative patterns, I now enjoy a new freedom in my relationship with others.

Several years ago, and ten years after receiving counseling, I sat down to write a letter to my father and mother listing the positive attributes I have experienced while living under their leadership. I thanked them and affirmed each positive attribute and special experience that I had the joy of receiving from them as their child.

What about the negative attributes? Over time, I had pruned them from my family orchard, one bad apple at a time. Therefore, this was no longer a necessary topic of discussion with my extended family.

Early on in my journey toward finding freedom from the negatives of my past I realized that forgiveness in an important form of pruning. I made the decision to forgive the people from my past who had caused me pain, left scars, or held me back from moving forward in a more positive life direction. Had those who caused me the pain asked for my forgiveness? No, it most cases they hadn't. Unfortunately, it's a rare thing for someone who has been hurtful to realize it and seek the forgiveness of those they've hurt. So, I made the "choice" to forgive the past. The moment I did, those past hurts no longer had power over me.

When we forgive someone for something they have done that caused us pain or offended us, we cut the cord in our souls that binds us to that past hurt and let it go. Therefore, there is no longer a reason to bring it up because it is no longer a part of our present. Psalm 103:12 says when God forgives us for our mistakes, He removes our rebellious acts as far away from us as the east is from the west. When we come into a relationship with God, He prunes away the negatives of our past. In doing so, the ability for the negatives of past generations to affect the lives of future generations is stopped. What a legacy to pass forward ... freedom through faith in God!

Once I embraced my freedom through faith I was able to forgive and prune, or remove, the negative and destructive traits from my past. They no longer are a part of my life today so they cannot be passed forward to future generations. Every pruning event needs to be done with care, but it does not require the permission of past generations.

My faith, my decision to forgive and remove the negatives of the past, and the act of affirming my parents' positive influences made a huge difference in my life. It has resulted in abundant blessing from God. Both of my children now have two parents who are affirming, encouraging, and speaking God's blessing over them daily.

Does the family orchard ever reach the point that the extended—and immediate—family trees no longer need pruning? The answer is no; just as seasons change and spring produces new growth and new fruit, our lives and journeys change and grow also.

The question then becomes, when the day arrives and my girls marry and sprout an immediate-family tree of their own, will they still need to prune the generational trees in the family orchard? Absolutely. Even though their mother and I are doing the best we know how to do to set a Godly example and impart Godly wisdom, we are still human and imperfect at times. However, it is comforting to know that even when we make mistakes as parents and leaders in our families, God is faithful. He will still do good in the lives of those in whom we have influence and impact.

This is my hope for you. With the growth of each new generational tree, may your family orchard grow stronger as you establish healthy relationships through consistent affirmation and encouragement of those you lead and influence. May the fruit produced by each newly rooted tree in your orchard positively impact many future generations. Here are some practical steps and insights for recording the family history.

Memorabilia

Most families have several boxes filled with bits of family history passed down from generation to generation. I happen to be the box-holder for my family. It contains hundreds of pictures of relatives from both sides of my parents' trees. It also includes marriage certificates, armed forces discharge papers, high school yearbooks, class rings, and letters from relatives of past generations.

In my experience, most families are overwhelmed with all this historical information and have no system in place by which to organize these items. Fortunately, there are several software applications available that make it easier to organize and maintain all the information by storing it in one place. Present generations should understand this is a vital part of keeping up with and transferring their families' heritage. Value must be placed upon understanding the importance of historical family information and how best to transfer it forward. That's why having scanned electronic copies of all pictures and documents is vital.

A great example of the power of memorabilia in influencing the lives of future generations is the shadow-box my parents put together for me that I keep on display in my office. It includes a picture of my great grandfather in his livery stable, a ring from the uncle after whom I was named, a thimble from my grandmother, and a watch and shaving blade from my grandfather.

This is a gift that means everything to me because it is something I cannot buy for myself from any store. It serves as a powerful reminder of the positive patterns and influences of past generations. It also encourages me to recognize that I have been given the opportunity to positively influence my family today as well as future generations to come. I often ask myself, what will my shadow box look like as it hangs on my children's wall? When they look at it, what impact will it represent in their lives?

When helping other families plan, I have seen meaningful furniture, quilts, jewelry, dishes, and tools transferred with love to the next generations. It is important to recognize that whatever memorabilia we have or will receive, it came from people who were called before us to have impact and influence on our lives.

What's In A Name?

As we saw in the chapter on family brands, a name attaches us to a specific family. It identifies the character, or "brand," of our family orchard. Your name is what people associate you with when they hear it spoken. When others hear my name, I want it to inspire thoughts of strong faith, honesty, and integrity. Take some time and give thought to the values you desire your name to inspire in the minds of others. As we move to the next chapter, you will have the opportunity to establish the family values by which you desire your family to be defined.

Understanding the heritage of your name is important as you continue to build upon it one generation at a time. You may be wondering if it is possible to change negative perceptions built up around a specific name. For some, the answer is "yes." For others, the truthful answer is "in time."

If the generations before you made poor life choices that ultimately created a negative legacy, you have the option to choose a different path in life and to establish better values by which to live moving forward. Time proves all things. The best advice I can give is: Live your life by such values that when people speak ill of you, no one will believe it. Remember the promise: "God has made everything beautiful for its own time. He has planted eternity in the human heart, but even so, people cannot see the whole scope of God's work from beginning to end" (Ecclesiastes 3:11 NLT).

In the movie *Christmas Vacation*, starring Chevy Chase as Clark Griswold, there is a scene that spoofs the Griswold's family Christmas traditions. Ellen Griswold's cousin Eddie shows up in a broken-down motorhome that he parks in the Griswold's front yard. Eddie is a Bubba from back in the woods and doesn't fit in with Clark's prestigious surroundings or the image he is working hard to portray. Eddie doesn't have a penny to his name and he continues to embarrass the entire family at all turns throughout the movie.

It is hilarious to watch the character of Eddie until you realize every family has an "Eddie Tree" in its orchard ... including yours. It may be a sibling, uncle, aunt, or cousin. The fruit on their tree not only looks bad it tastes bad too. It is embarrassing when others converse with you about fruity "Eddie." Family members like Eddie often adopt values of their own for their lives that need to be pruned away and discarded.

When your family's name is tainted by current or previous generations, what do you do? You prune. Decide what values, belief systems, character traits, and disciplines you want to instill today that can be transferred to the next generation tomorrow. It is like establishing an orchard, one tree at a time. The root system you establish today will grow a strong tree with healthy fruit that will sprout new vibrant trees from season to season for generations to come.

Break the cycle. Start a new, better cycle.

Traditions

It's important to remember, cherish, and follow key traditions for the sake of future generations. Many a weekend night, while growing up, I was involved in table games of cards, Monopoly, and Stratego with my family. The night included popcorn and maybe a western movie that would entertain us all. I continue this family tradition with my wife and daughters. Game night is a highlight in our home and gives us opportunity to connect as a family.

To this day, another family tradition that continues to influence who I am today is the camping trips we experienced as kids—travelling to forty-two states over the years. Every summer we loaded our travel trailer and set out on a journey to see the beautiful landscapes of our country and experience its history across different regions of America. I was blessed to enjoy many of the state parks and all of the National Parks with my family.

Today, I continue to share this simple but powerful tradition with my immediate family. It has brought moments of unique experiences and family bonding. Whatever your family traditions, it is important to identify the ones that bring meaning and connectedness to your family. Sit down together with your family and choose a handful of traditions from the different extended trees in your family orchard that have had meaning to you and continue to incorporate the fruit of those traditions into your family's future. These moments represent golden apples whose taste you don't want to forget ... or fail to share.

FAMILY HERITAGE IN THE FUTURE

Your family heritage influences who you are and how you live out your life today. Maintaining your heritage enables future generations to see the wisdom, leadership, values, and influence of previous generations. In the sections that follow I will share some ways to effectively keep the treasures of the past secure so future generations may celebrate them.

FAMILY HISTORIAN

Every family needs to have an identified person who can receive and transfer important family information to the next generation. The best candidate is the family member who possesses strong organizational skills as well as an interest in keeping this information and memorabilia together.

Great websites such as familytreemaker.com and ancestry.com can aid you in locating, researching, and communicating with other trees from your family orchard. I encourage you to explore these helpful sites, keeping in mind that some do require a fee for the services.

Automation is essential for effectively handling all the information from our histories. Once the family history is fleshed out, it is easy to maintain on an ongoing basis by using one of the tools mentioned above. The family historian is encouraged to update each family member periodically as new historical information is discovered or added.

There should be an ongoing recruiting process to identify the next family historian. Engage young children or grandchildren in the activity of organizing and recording the family history. Not only can it be fun for them, but it is an educational process as well. Think how fun it could be for a child interested in history to study academic history while following his or her family history at the same time. It helps to make the events of the past come alive!

LEVERAGING TECHNOLOGY

In my experience, preserving key family documents is the most frustrating and cumbersome task for families to manage. There are many programs available online to help you resolve this issue. Some programs feature a private virtual vault system, which allows you to securely store your personal information.

Other features could include a data management system that incorporates multi-level security with compliance retention, and 24/7 immediate and secure accesses to documents through any internet connection. A program like this could help eliminate the need to travel to a bank location during hours of operation. It would also enable someone to add information directly from their technology source, and send information like medical records, tax returns, legal documents, and the like to a professional advisor, attorney, service provider, medical facility or family member.

In addition to the features mentioned above, this type of service could also provide a prime spot to scan and store family photos, memorabilia, and any other family history in this safe environment. Any new memorabilia documentation can be added as needed. Instead of huge boxes that can be stolen, lost or destroyed, your memories and historical documentation would be persevered safely for future generations.

VIDEOGRAPHY

The use of videography is a great way to maintain family history for future generations. It enables families to see and hear the patriarch and matriarch of the family actually tell the stories and communicate their life experiences. Given that a large percentage of the population is made up of visual learners, videography is an effective tool in communicating and transitioning the past into the future. Great-great grandchildren who never physically met the family's patriarch and matriarch can still build a strong connection and feel directly influenced by them through the medium of video. Have fun making the family videos. Make it a family affair by inviting younger generations from the extended family to ask questions about values, beliefs, or experiences that the patriarch or matriarch of the family can answer.

You may choose to set up your own talk show format appointing a family host and asking the older members of the family to be the guests on the show with the remaining family members filling in as audience members. This is a great activity to incorporate into family reunions. The more family that get involved in shooting the video, the more fun and rewarding the experience can be. Think of the impact the process will make on the lives involved as well as those who will watch the video in the years to come.

DEFINING YOUR FAMILY HERITAGE

We have discussed a few of the ways to effectively participate in impacting your family's heritage. This information will help you in the pruning process—when you have all of the information gathered that you can, you and your family can make decisions about what traits to keep and what to flush out. But remember, it takes time, intentionality, and effort for an apple tree to produce great fruit. And so it is in growing a strong and vibrant family tree!

You have the opportunity to claim the promise of a strong spiritual heritage through the lineage of Abraham when you enter into a relationship with God through faith. Whatever your generational heritage may look like, your goal should be to establish a legacy to pass forward that reflects a strong spiritual heritage and incorporates the best attributes and patterns from past generations. Why? The next generation deserves our best. Even though we may not have received it, we have an opportunity to give it.

RECAP

1. There is strength in vulnerability and revealing brokenness. Share all of your experiences. Heal generational wounds and give your heirs the healthiest legacy you can.
2. Decide what you want to nurture, grow, expand, and give to the next generation and decide what you need to prune from your generational line so that it dies with your generation and does not get passed forward.
3. It is vital to your legacy to create and implement a process for recording your history and appoint a family historian that understands the importance of carrying on the call.

CHAPTER TEN

WHO ARE YOU?

"People can't live with change if there's not a changeless core
inside them. The key to the ability to change is a changeless
sense of who you are, what you are about and what you value."
—Stephen R. Covey

ESTABLISHED CORE VALUES are the seed from which every family tree grows. Determining your core values is the single most important step to establishing a family plan. Core values can be defined as a personal code of ethics that guides the decisions you make.

It is important not to confuse establishing core values with setting goals. Values are not goals because it is impossible to "reach" a value. You live in accordance with a value. When you reach a goal, you set a new one. But you never reach a value—therefore you never require a new one. Again, values represent the seed from which your family tree takes root and grows. There are several major life categories that are affected by our established core values: family, vision, relationships, and management of our finances. Your core values drive the legacy you create and pass forward to future generations.

We are called by God to impact the lives of others. With that in mind let's look again at Lot, Abraham's nephew. As you'll recall, Abraham gave Lot the first opportunity to choose the land he wanted to keep for himself. After Lot looked over all the available land he determined that the section of land to the east was the best. It was green and lush and looked like the Garden of Eden.

He made a split-second decision. Lot didn't really take the time to think about Uncle Abraham and what might be best for him. Lot thought only about what was best for Lot. Talk about an entitlement mentality! But Lot may have thought he deserved the better land; after all, his life had not been absent of its own challenges.

I have certainly observed this entitlement mindset over the many years I've spent working with families through the decision-making process. Sadly, this entitled attitude fractures many family trees. The heirs place value on the wrong things. Interestingly enough, that is exactly how the story played out for Lot and his family. The land he chose and thought was so valuable eventually became a wasteland we know today as two of the most corrupt places in history—Sodom and Gomorrah.

Lot looked at the beauty to assess the value of the land rather than looking at the potential of the land to grow and build future success. He didn't take time to consider all of his options and how they might affect not only his life but the future of his family. He was focused on claiming the best and dealing later with the rest.

Lot's entitlement and greed nearly cost him not only his entire fortune but also his life. He placed value on the wrong things. Pursuing the wrong values led him to make a decision that would negatively affect the rest of his life and the lives of future generations as well. This is why establishing your core values is so important. When difficult decisions come along in life, and they will, strong values give you a reliable yardstick against which to measure your decisions.

FOLLOW YOUR COMPASS

If you have ever climbed a "fourteener" (a mountain with a summit higher than fourteen-thousand feet), you know the importance of taking a compass along for the hike. In some cases it can mean the difference between life and death. The purpose of the compass is to give you direction, to help you keep your bearings as you hike through disorienting, treacherous places. It points you in the right direction. No matter where you stand on the mountain, you can hold a compass in your hand and it will point North. The higher you climb, the more steep the drops. The climate and weather elements get more extreme and change abruptly, sometimes making visibility very difficult. Too many steps in the wrong direction and you end up lost, hurt, or worse.

Life is the same way. It is a journey that is walked more successfully with a clear sense of direction. Establishing your core values gives you a compass to navigate the journey of life. Your life values determine the direction of your choices moving forward. They give you a defined sense of purpose and a predetermined course to travel.

TRUE NORTH

True north refers to the North Pole. Some traditional compasses are calibrated to a magnetic north located in northern Canada. True maps are calibrated to true north. This means that traditional compasses must be recalibrated a few degrees from magnetic north in order to point to true north depending on the location of the person using the compass.

When a magnetic compass is used, it always needs to be recalibrated to true north or the user will end up in the wrong place.

Through my upbringing and training as an Eagle Scout, I had a great foundation from which to establish my own personal core values. But I have to admit—as I entered the business world, I lost my focus and moved away from the values I had established for my life. Soon, I viewed them with a-rear-view-mirror mentality. They were something from my past but I was not looking to them to measure the decisions affecting my then present nor my future. This lack of focus caused me to value achievements and success more than driving my character and values to a deeper level.

Without those bearings, I was making decisions out of necessity, convenience, and desire, instead of what was true, just, and moral. Everything was relative and changed according to my circumstances at the time. My guiding force—my compass—was never recalibrated properly to true north. I was stuck at the compass' default position, lost, and living my life according to the world's standards.

So many of us fall victim to a performance-based or convenience-based value system. When this happens, we are driven by our competitive natures and our need for "stuff." This causes our goals to revolve around material goods and worldly status instead of what is truly good.

A person with a faulty compass may not identify this view of life as a problem. You may be wondering right now how someone with strong established core values lets this happen. Chances are they never saw it coming. Their compass wasn't recalibrated to true north—a position of true value and worth.

Working with individuals from all walks of life, I have talked with some who started out with non-negotiable core values as the anchor for their lives. However, somewhere along the way they drifted from their anchor—increasingly allowing the opinions of others to influence the decisions they made. I began to wonder how this happened. I realized that often the legacy a leader desires is never established when the core values they are actually living out aren't pointing to their hoped-for destination. The compass is off. To map out a successful journey in life, the first step is to recalibrate the compass to true north. We do this by identifying, defining, and claiming our core values for life.

If you're like many people I know, and how I used to be, you haven't really thought deeply about establishing and naming your core values. Many people live life more randomly than they'd like to admit. Decision-making without a focused stance in life is usually a symptom of relativism—an ever-changing flow of *"whatever feels good for the moment."*

CALIBRATING YOUR COMPASS

The following exercise has proven to be a valuable tool in helping me determine my core values. It is designed to help you identify, claim, and establish a set of core values (guiding principles) for your life. These values become your compass and a key part of your legacy.

Begin by taking some time to read and seriously think about the questions I am about to ask. Use the chart I provide to record your answers to the questions.

To help you with your answers use this as a qualifying test: Think about someone taking that value away from you or limiting your access to it. How does that make you feel? If there are no strong emotions associated with the thought of someone taking that value or principle from you, then you need to dig deeper and find the values that are most important to you, the ones about which you are passionate.

Keep in mind your answers are just that ... *your* answers. They are unique to you. To help you with your answers, I have provided a list of possible core values on the following pages you may choose from, or you may come up with a value that is not on the list. There are no wrong answers.

Now let's get started with the questions:

QUESTION	ANSWER
1. What two words "best" describe the essence of your character?	
2. What two values are most important to you?	
3. What two adjectives do you most want others to use when defining your character?	
4. When thinking of your children and heirs, what are the two most important values you want to pass forward to them?	
5. What are the two most important values you look for in a person when establishing your inner circle of friends?	
6. List one or two words that best define the non-negotiable principles you stand for above all else in life.	
7. What two words best define the person you respect most in your life?	
8. For what (not whom) would you be willing to lay down your life?	

Now that you have answered the questions, the next step is to prioritize your values. You do this by narrowing down your answers to your top six or eight. These become your core values moving forward.

POTENTIAL CORE VALUES

Accountability	Grace	Peace
Diligence	Gratitude	Purity
Discipline	Honesty	Respect
Encouragement	Humility	Self-Control
Excellence	Integrity	Selflessness
Faith	Joy	Faithfulness
Forgiveness	Kindness	Temperance
Generosity	Love	Service
Gentleness	Loyalty	Trustworthiness
Goodness	Patience	Creativity
Chastity	Compassion	Authenticity
Honor	Virtue	Wisdom

CLAIMING YOUR VALUES

You have probably heard the phrase, "Name it and Claim it." Now that you have named them it is time to claim them as your personal framework around which to build your generational home as well as establish your legacy.

First, your core values are not just principles or standards by which to live, they define the principles and standards you choose to live out. They shape your character and help you shape the character of your family. So much so, that they become the essence of your legacy.

For me personally, one of my core values is faith. I desire to live a life that reflects the essence of God in all I do. Simply naming faith as one of my values will not get me to my final goal of living a Christ-like life. I now have to claim it as one of my identifying values. Then I must put effort and intention into becoming a person of faith.

It is important to understand that core values do not change over time. They are not temporal. Core values actually perpetuate and direct your time, effort, intentions, and actions. They are an unwavering force that acts as a litmus test for everything you do. They drive your goals, your sense of right and wrong, what you believe, and how you think, act, and speak. They ultimately drive your purpose and help you define the principles you stand for as you interact with and impact others.

Now that you have claimed your core values you must align them with your actions. This enables you to make a significant difference in your home, family, community, and your future.

CHARTING YOUR COURSE

How do you chart your course in accordance with your core values? You begin by writing out an action statement. This statement defines what you will accomplish or achieve with each value or trait. For example, let's look at one of my core values ... integrity. I took a piece of paper and listed my eight core values, integrity being number one. Next to integrity I wrote, "I will be known as a man who chooses to stand on and stand up for what is right in every area of my life, regardless of the consequences, or who, if anyone, is watching." I continued down my page writing my personal action statement after each core value.

Using the following chart, list your six to eight core values in the left-hand column. Next to each core value write out your personal action statement in the right-hand column.

CORE VALUE	ACTION STATEMENT

Refer often to this list until you have memorized your core values and corresponding action statements. They will help keep you accountable as you chart the course in your daily life.

Will you fall short at times? Yes. No one is perfect. We can't be. However, putting our thoughts on paper commits them to mind. Our minds then translate our desired outcomes into corresponding action. Our actions are driven by our core values and out of those core values flow the principles by which we live.

A journey without an accurate chart will surely fail. But a well-charted course will lead to a life of significance.

CONNECTING TO ACCOUNTABILITY

Connecting to someone who will hold you accountable as you walk out your well-charted course is of great importance. These individuals serve to empower and encourage you, as well as to challenge you at times along your journey.

Look for individuals in your life who share your same values—people you respect. They may be your age or older. I encourage you to stay within your same gender. It may be a family member, friend, colleague, but it needs to be someone you trust and who has proven to be trustworthy.

Be specific in what you are asking them to do. Explain that you are establishing a life plan and want them to hold you accountable as you walk through putting your core values into action. Decide together the best way to make this work in your relationship. It may be connecting for coffee once a week or monthly. Make sure the other person understands your expectations and that you understand theirs. This helps to alleviate any disappointments in the future.

Here are a few questions you may consider giving your mentor as an accountability checklist as he or she walks this course alongside you:

1. Discuss your media habits. What are you watching on TV? What are you looking at on the Internet? What magazines and books are you reading? What are you listening to on the radio? How much time are you spending and who are you talking to on Facebook or other social media sites?
2. How well does your calendar or schedule reflect your core values?
3. How would your spouse, children, parents, close friends, or work

associates say you are living out each core value in your daily decisions and life actions?

4. What does your checkbook, credit card statement, or budget say about each of your core values?

5. How closely aligned are each of your core values when compared to your daily lifestyle?

Leonardo da Vinci said, "He who loves practice without theory is like the sailor who boards a ship without a rudder and compass and never knows where he may cast." Mentors, advisors, or accountability partners are important in life. What good is a ship if it has no map to direct it, no ocean to move it, no captain to steer it, and no navigator to guide it to its final destination?

COMPLETING YOUR LEGACY

As you walk out your core values in your everyday life, it is important to assess how you are doing at different points along the journey. Focusing on these four areas of your life—family, professional, spiritual, and social—each month take a quick assessment of how your actions are aligning with your core values. Be aware of areas that need improving. The first step to recalibrating your compass if you get off course is recognizing you are moving in the wrong direction. The sooner you see and admit you are drifting off course the quicker you can make positive adjustments.

We are all works-in-progress. However, by establishing and living out your core values in every single area of your life you are charting a course that will result in one awesome journey!

Those things that you truly value in life are the very things that give you value through life. They define your legacy!

TRANSFERRING YOUR FAMILY VALUES

Once you have identified and established the core values that represent who you are as a family, how do you transfer those values to the next generation? There is a saying I heard my parents quote many times throughout my life and I'm sure you've heard it too. "Actions speak louder than words." You live out your values for others to see.

People watch what you do and then decide what they choose to hear. Live a life that points others toward God. You don't have to be perfect, but you do have to be real. You pass your family values forward one choice, one action, one word at a time. When you live a life of transparency and walk out the values that really matter, you will build and transfer a legacy that will withstand the test of time. And that my friend, is transferring a transformative legacy to future generations!

RECAP

1. Identifying your core values gives you a direction to go when faced with decisions, big and small.
2. All decisions of life should be measured through the filter of your core values. If the opportunities do not align, your decision will be easy to make.
3. Your core values should direct your time, effort, intentions, and actions.

CHAPTER ELEVEN

CLARIFY YOUR VISION

"Vision is really about focus; it requires setting your eyes on
the summit while standing at the base of the trail, and then
establishing the best route to conquer it." —Jim Rohn

W E MUST UNDERSTAND VISION is important because it provides
you with focus and direction as you move forward through life.
If you have not established specific and clearly defined goals you are
not going to realize the maximum potential that lies within you. Vision
paints a picture in your mind that will determine the type of life you live.

Zig Ziglar puts it this way, "In a sense, your vision sets the limits and
defines the boundaries of your success potential. It is never the other way
around. Your vision, not your success potential, defines how far you can
go and what you can achieve."[1]

It is also important to ask yourself this question: Is your vision positive
or negative? Do you picture yourself as God sees you? And where does

---

[1] Ziglar, Zig. *See You at the Top.* 25th ed. Pelican Publishing, 2010.

God see you? When you focus on God's results for your life you will see your vision move toward reality. God promises us that He knows the plans He has for us to give us hope and a future and not to bring us harm. He challenges us to ask Him about the things we do not know, the direction He has for our lives, and He will show us and make our plans succeed (see Jeremiah 29:11, 33:3).

What are your motivating factors in life? Personally, my first and foremost motivating factor is my faith in God. Next, are my wife and children. Followed by, I would say, my work, along with giving to the needs of others.

Once you identify your motivating factors you are better able to establish a vision. As the leader of your family, it is important that you establish a vision with and for your family unit. It is also vital that you communicate the vision.

GOD GIVES ABRAHAM VISION

We call Abraham "father" not because he got God's attention by living like a saint, but because God made something out of Abraham when he was a nobody. In Scripture, God says to Abraham, "I set you up as father of many nations." Abraham was first named "father" and then became a father because he dared to trust the vision God had given him.

He trusted God to do what only God could do: raise the dead to life, with a word make something out of nothing. When everything was hopeless, Abraham believed anyway, deciding to live not on the basis of what he saw he couldn't do but on what God said he would do. And so he was made father of a multitude of peoples. God himself said to him, "You're going to have a big family, Abraham!"

Abraham didn't focus on his own impotence and say, "It's hopeless. This hundred-year-old body could never father a child." Nor did he survey Sarah's decades of infertility and give up. He didn't tiptoe around God's promise asking cautiously skeptical questions. He plunged into the promise and came up strong, ready for God, sure that God would make good on what he had said. That's why it is said, "Abraham was declared fit before God by trusting God to set him right." (Romans 4:19-25 *The Message*)

It is amazing to see that God didn't just give Abraham a promise and vision; He gave Abraham a picture of what was to come. He told Abraham to look at the stars in the sky as if they literally represented in number the nations that God would establish for him to father. The stars were too many to count. God gave Abraham a physical reminder, a *vision* of his faithfulness to come.

It's not just Abraham God gave vision to. He also gives vision to us! But, we must first embrace and believe the One who brought Jesus to life when the conditions in the world seemed equally hopeless as they do today. The sacrifice of Jesus made us fit for God, set us *right with God*. And it is this same God who directs our vision to the place of real reality—not our *perceived* reality.

PUTTING VISION INTO THE FAMILY PLAN

New Year's Day happens once every year. With it comes the same question, "What is your New Year's resolution?"

Typical answers are things like losing weight, spending more time with family, saving more money, or becoming more involved in the community. These are all great resolutions but may I suggest one other? How about providing such a clear vision for your family that all future generations will understand the purpose, passion, and impact for their family tree?

The first step in creating a family plan is establishing core values; the second step is determining vision. Part of the process of establishing vision is determining what impact your family wants to make.

Our lives and the lives of those within our families will tend to follow the direction of our vision. Remember life is not always fair, but God is! God does not cancel His plan because of our disappointments. Look again at Abraham. God set a vision in place for Abraham's future before He blessed him with a son to pass the vision to future generations.

God essentially said, "Look again, at the stars, Abraham. Trust Me with your age, your impotence, with Sarah's infertility, with the hopelessness you feel. I *will* make you the father of all nations. Look at the stars when your vision seems lost."

We are promised in Psalm 30:5, "Weeping may endure for the night but *joy* comes in the morning" (NKJV). Why morning? Maybe because it is easier to see after the sun has risen, so we have clearer vision through the "Son's light."

WHAT'S PICTURED IN YOUR FRAME?

My wife loves to decorate our home with framed pictures. Pictures of past vacations, friends, family members, and our girls' pictures through different stages of life adorn our walls. They provide us with visual reminders of special moments, friends, and things we love.

From time to time, my wife, Tamera, replaces the pictures in the frames with new ones. I will look toward a frame and realize the image inside of it has changed. It causes me to focus on something different, a different memory or moment in time.

Vision is a picture framed by possibility. It is a visual image of where we are going—the direction we are moving. A moment. A place. A mission we are moving toward accomplishing. What is in the frame of your vision? Your life will not change until you change your vision—your picture. Joel Osteen puts it this way: "Your life will follow your vision."

Once you accomplish one step toward reaching your vision as a family, put new pictures in your frames! Capture the steps you take in accomplishing your vision. When you move toward God's call you will see your vision move from possibility to reality! Remember, "If you can see the invisible, God can do the impossible," Joel Osteen reminds us.

NO VISION IS TOO GREAT TO ACCOMPLISH

Life will try to put out your internal fire as it moves toward external greatness. Make your vision big enough to let faith and favor be necessary. God's vision for your family is greater than any dream your family can dream.

Sometimes our environment holds us back. This reminds me of a story about a tadpole hatched in the water of a well. The tadpole grew into a frog and was so happy in its little well. The frog swam and jumped and found contentment in the small space.

One day the frog grew large enough and climbed up the wall of the well. Once at the top it popped open the lid to the well and noticed a pond close by. The frog grew unhappy with the well and soon jumped from the well and hopped to the pond. The frog was happy in the pond, swimming and jumping in the water.

Until one day, curiosity got the best of the frog and it hopped down a path leading away from the pond. There the frog discovered a big river. No longer content with the smaller pond the frog jumped into the river and decided to stay. Again the frog was happy in the river, jumping and swimming in the water each day.

However, it wasn't long until a boat came near the frog and the frog hopped on board. The boat travelled down the river and into the ocean. The frog saw the ocean and was overcome with joy. It hopped from the boat to make the ocean its home. "Finally," the frog thought, "I have found a place to thrive with no limits!"

Break out of the well of confinement and move toward the ocean of limitless possibility. Create an atmosphere of victory for your family. Get out of your comfort zone together as a family, building one another up as you move together to accomplish your vision.

The place you choose to live defines your ultimate destiny. Choose to live in an atmosphere of victory. Create an inspiring environment where your family feels they are in a place where they can achieve the impossible.

Proverbs 29:18 says we are limited by a lack of vision. Just like Abraham, God will give you a vision that is too big to accomplish on your own. Why? God wants to be a part of your vision. He wants you to set a vision for your family that requires His faithfulness in order to accomplish it. This is the greatest gift you can give your family—helping to establish a vision that requires and reveals God's faithfulness.

RECAP

1. We must understand our choice is between the vision of the world that will enslave us and the vision of God that provides us with the freedom we seek.

2. Your family needs to not only be aware of your vision for them, but they also need to be an intricate part of the plan in seeing that vision play out.

3. Don't limit your vision to only what you feel is humanly possible in one lifetime. Remember, God puts His "super" on your "natural" and there are amazing things that can take place in your lifetime if you choose to work *with* the one who created you.

CHAPTER TWELVE

WE NEED OTHERS

"Positive relationships are like a healthy tree, they demand
attention and care in the beginning but once they blossom,
they provide you shade in all situations of life."
—Unknown

RELATIONSHIPS ARE ONE OF THE MOST IMPORTANT aspects of a
person's life. We owe much of who we are today to the influences
of the people who crossed our paths throughout our lives as well as the
influences within our family unit.

The truth is the influence of others has a lot to do with how we view
ourselves and what we become as people. Relationships with others make
us feel as though we belong to something. We were created with a desire
for fellowship with one another. Our value systems, visions, goals for the
future, and sense of security and stability are shaped by the influence
of our families as well as the friendships and associations we have with
others. They help to define our worldview and the perspective from which
we see things. We all have our own individual talents, gifts, goals, and

dreams yet are also a part of a collective whole. We are each unique and special having our own one-of-a-kind fingerprint.

Looking for a minute at just the family unit, each has its own unique collective personality, or as we established, a brand. There are two-parent families, stepfamilies, single-parent families, and the list goes on. Some families get along great while others barely speak. Some families are large in number. Others are small. The common element that all families share is relationships within their unit. And with relationship comes responsibility.

RELATIONSHIPS THEN AND NOW

We have looked at a lot of things about Abraham's life up to this point. One thing that stands out to me as I look at his journey is that Abraham was a family man. He understood the importance of nurturing well the relationships within his family unit, both immediate and extended. He took his call seriously by first being a good father at home. God saw his faithfulness and blessed him greatly by making him the father of many nations.

Like Abraham, I totally understand the rewards as well as the challenges of parenting. I can now relate to stepping into the patriarchal role in the extended family. Seven years after Tamera and I were married, we decided it was time to enlarge our family of two. After several months passed with no success, we started down the track of testing and research with fertility specialists. Unbeknownst to us, this was the beginning of a six-year journey.

Toward the end of the six years, we realized the odds of us achieving pregnancy were not in our favor. With both of us now being over forty we understood the dream of having children might not be in our future. And then, just as God spoke the words to Abraham, the words we longed to hear were finally spoken to us: "You are expecting a baby!"

God worked a miracle for Tamera and me. Through answered prayer,

He increased the size of our family. We held our first child, a little girl, in our arms, followed seventeen months later by our second daughter. Both were miracle babies who made us parents.

Over the years, I've noticed many families share a similar experience. As couples are waiting longer to start their families, a new generation is emerging known as the "sandwich generation." The sandwich generation refers to those who are raising young children while taking care of aging parents at the same time. The experiences I have observed through all stages of my life—being parents, having children, and with my clients—have allowed God to prepare my heart for the journey. I am currently walking as a member of this newly defined generation.

I believe we are called to honor our parents. God commands us to honor our fathers and mothers so that we'll live a long time in the land God has given us. Helping our aging parents is not always easy. Neither is raising our young children into responsible adults. My dad passed away several years ago, and while my wife and I are raising our two young daughters we are also helping with my mother's and mother-in-law's care. I am blessed to have two great moms but I understand this is not the experience for everyone. Yet, whatever the case may be, we are all called to honor our parents.

Let me be very clear about a few things here. Honoring your parents does not mean agreeing with everything they do. Honoring your parents means caring for them as God cares for you and respecting their position in your life. Some parents have made decisions that are not honorable or respectable. You don't have to honor and respect what they say, said, do, or did—but you do need to respect and honor them as your earthly mom and dad.

Many in the sandwich generation will understand what I mean when I say we are all learning patience and how to exercise the strongest communication and relational skills we can muster as we forge this path largely untraveled until now.

The truth is the family you grew up with had a profound impact on how you relate and communicate with every other person you come into contact with today. Some of you were blessed to see great communication and relational skills modeled in front of you. Others may have experienced the opposite.

Understanding the lessons of your past explains much about the reality of your present. However, where you go from here and how you manage the relationships in your life are totally up to you! If you haven't had the best relationship with your parents up to this point, maybe you can use this time in the later years of their lives to start building a stronger bridge for your children to cross over.

Communicating your feelings and perspectives with the older gener-ations and asking them to communicate their feelings and perspectives to you is where healing begins. Sometimes the greatest words we can communicate are, "I'm sorry," and "I forgive you." When these words are spoken, a healthier relationship is forged.

Your children are watching how you care for your parents. One day, before you know it, they will be caring for you. They learn to honor others by observation, not through explanation or instruction.

If you are sandwiched, like me, between two generations, may love, honor, kindness, faithfulness, joy, and patience fill the space between your generational bread! There you have a sandwich worth having for many generations to come!

Abraham, also like me, being an older father, was most likely taking care of elderly family members as well and had probably taken the baton assuming the leadership role within his extended family. Not only had Abraham learned to be a great dad to Isaac and son to Terah, he learned how to be the patriarchal leader for all his family and a role model for generations to come.

INFLUENCING THE MASSES

Not only are we called to be positive influencers within our families, we are called to influence others outside of our family units. Like it or not people watch what we do every day. We all lead others somewhere and the final destination depends upon where we are going and how we are choosing to get there. Basically, we are all given an incredible opportunity to mentor the people around us. What exactly is mentorship?

I believe mentoring is two-fold—intentional and unintentional. Intentional mentorship happens when you commit to "do-life" with another person. Helping them walk through the ups and downs of their day-to-day journey. It is a mutual relationship built on trust. You are agreeing to speak wisdom and truth into the life of another person. They in turn are willing to receive what you have to give. Intentional mentoring is a two-way street. As you walk alongside someone else, they will also hold you accountable in your talk and walk. Remember you cannot lead someone beyond the place you are yourself. As you help others reach the heights of God's call in their lives, make sure you also have someone speaking into your life as well.

Unintentional mentorship is when others look to you for guidance and wisdom and you may not even be aware they are watching or listening. This is why it is so important that your yes be yes, and your no be no. Social media has made this more important than ever. With Twitter feeds moving a mile a minute, Facebook posts multiplying by the second and mobile apps so widely available, messages now spread like a wildfire. Your influence is much broader than you think! Social media has widened and broadened our circles of influence beyond comprehension. Live and communicate with positive actions and words because whether or not you're intentionally mentoring someone in your circle of influence, I guarantee you are unintentionally mentoring someone in your circle of influence. So communicate with Godly intention in everything you say and do! You have the power to change lives! How and what you communicate is the key!

RUNNING WITH THE PACK

I have experienced the power of communication firsthand! Let me begin this story by saying, "Being the person in front of the pack is not only difficult, but, at times downright scary!" Over the holidays, my family witnessed this truth up close and personally. We, along with several other families, took a dogsled ride in the beautiful mountains of Montana on a crisp, sunny December morning. Dressed in our warmest winter gear, we drove out into the middle of the wilderness to the location of the sledder's home. His property backed up to thousands of acres of state-owned land upon which he has spent years creating and grooming dog trails.

The land provides an eleven mile track of snow-covered trails that enable him to properly hone the skills of his dogs. The average dog weighed forty to fifty pounds. The pack had 121 dogs. We could hear the ensemble of barks and howls from the moment we exited our car. What I didn't realize was that we were about to experience teamwork and communication at the highest levels.

The master sledder appeared with four sleds ready to handle the morning jaunt. At first glance it was obvious the sled dogs knew it was time to perform. A pack totaling nine pulled my sled, with a mom and daughter in front and seven eager teammates following close behind. We noticed immediately that the lead dogs served their master brilliantly. Their effortless stride seemed endless as they pulled my oldest daughter and me on the eleven-mile journey in one hour.

The pack worked in unison as they listened to and obeyed the call commands of their master as he provided direction to the lead dog. The pack followed the commands willingly. The master sledder, lead dogs, and pack worked together like a hand in a glove, communicating in perfect harmony through signals and calls. As we traveled over the miles all we could hear were the commands of the master and the paws of the pack working together in unison. Although they did indeed run to follow their leader, more importantly, they ran for the affirmation of the sled master.

As we pulled into the yard and the sled came to a halt, the sled master poured his affirmation upon his pack. He was a man of small stature yet he communicated with grandeur his gratitude, extending praises, and giving treats, hugs, and kisses to his nine faithful followers. The sled master represents the alpha male. The dogs were rewarded handsomely for their devotion as their master provided abundant affection and all the provisions necessary to more than meet their needs.

There will come a time in most of our lives to assume the role of leader within our families and circles of influence. We, in a sense, become the sled masters. It is our responsibility to provide guidance, direction, and wisdom to those in our sphere of influence, our pack. How we view that responsibility is paramount to the level of success we will achieve as the leader and chief communicator of our pack. As a manager of the assets and people God has placed under our authority, we are responsible to be faithful and diligent in the management of not only our family relationships but the relationships God gives us with others too.

If you want to be an effective leader, you must be willing to serve the masses as well as follow and submit to the direction your master leads. The best leaders are great followers. You notice in the story, the lead dogs followed the sled master and at the same time they led the dogs who followed closely behind them. Learning to effectively communicate with others is the key to creating a healthy environment full of respect and love for one another.

THE VALUE OF POSITIVE COMMUNICATION

As we talked about before, positive communication is the key to building healthy relationships. Whatever your circle of influence may look like, from family to friends to business associates and beyond, it takes time and effort to build positive relationships.

Research shows that people who experience positive communication throughout their lives have higher self-esteem, decreased substance abuse, and suffer from less anxiety and depression.

For positive communication to occur, everyone must feel comfortable sharing their needs, wishes, and concerns in an honest and trusting environment without fear of rejection. The sooner this environment is created the more open others will be to sharing the everyday events and circumstances of their lives. We all desire a soft place to fall.

Strong communication skills open the doors of opportunity. By modeling positive communication skills as well as creating an environment that encourages positive communication, you are passing a lasting legacy forward to future generations. Through your actions you teach others how to effectively communicate with those in their spheres of influence.

STRENGTHENING RELATIONSHIPS WITH OTHERS

There are several things we do as members of my family that not only strengthen our relationships with one another but also help our children strengthen their relationships with others. We work to model strong communication skills by nurturing our relationships with one another. From the time my daughters were old enough to enjoy a night out with their dad, I have made Daddy-daughter date nights a regular priority. One such night in particular stands out in my mind. My oldest daughter and I went to dinner followed by a trip to a Barnes and Noble bookstore. We ran into a friend of my daughter's who was also out enjoying some time with her dad.

We talked with them for a while and toward the end of the conversation the friend's dad asked if my daughter could come home with them and sleep over. I explained that we were on a date and another night would be better. My daughter was frustrated with me and let me know it.

After the friend and her dad left, my daughter and I finished browsing through the bookstore and then walked back to my truck to make the drive home. She continued to give me the silent treatment for the first few minutes of our journey. Then she said, "You know what Daddy? I think I know the reason why you didn't want me to spend the night with my friend tonight." I said, "Really, what do you think it was?" She said, "It's because you are a planner isn't it?" I thought about her observation for a minute before explaining that was actually a part of it.

She went on to tell me she had noticed I like to plan and don't care much for surprises. She is exactly right. I am a planner. I clarified my reasoning to her that while I prefer an advanced invitation, it more had to do with the fact that I didn't want to share our date night with others. We had planned to spend the evening hanging out with one another and she was a blessing to me and I valued her and our time together. I could tell by the smile on her face she understood and appreciated the decision I made to decline the invitation of her friend.

My daughter learned some very important things through this experience. She learned her dad values her. She learned when others value you they give you their time and attention. She learned what it means to extend value to others. My daughter also learned to value family relationships and how to balance that with the value for friendships.

Time spent on trivial things at the expense of time spent on things that matter is time you can never get back. Make one-on-one time for the people who matter in your life. Relationships are priceless and pay dividends of blessings in the years to come.

Make it your goal to nurture your relationships because: "From the fruit of his lips a man is filled with good things" (Proverbs 12:14 NIV).

REALLY, GOD?

One of the greatest stories of faith was when God called Abraham to sacrifice his son. This son is the same miracle gift through whom God promised Abraham all of his heirs would come. The covenant Abraham made with God could only continue through Isaac.

How did Abraham handle this difficult call? He saddled up a donkey, grabbed two servants and Isaac, and headed up the mountain to the place of sacrifice. It was about a fifty mile, three-day journey.

I don't know about you, but if God told me to sacrifice my miracle child I think I would negotiate with God to take my life instead. But Abraham didn't flinch when God spoke to him. What I find interesting is when they reached the top of the mountain Isaac asked Abraham where the sheep was they were to sacrifice. I cannot imagine the heaviness of Abraham's heart as he watched his son carrying the wood the final steps up the mountain on which he would sacrifice his son.

Abraham told Isaac, "God Himself will provide the sheep." He then prepared the altar and bound Isaac placing him on top of the wood. Abraham raised his knife to kill his son as a sacrifice when at that very moment God sent an angel to stop him. Abraham looked up the mountain and saw a ram provided by God that became the sacrifice in Isaac's place.

Abraham's faith in God was strong and unwavering. His obedience brought pleasure to God. Before Abraham and Isaac made their journey back down the mountain toward home, God blessed Abraham and every descendent that would follow, including you and me.

Abraham understood by faith that God was the provider and protector of everything in his life including his child. When you as the leader of your family surrender your pack to the care and leadership of the Master, you will see God's blessing and favor poured out over your family. Surrender ushers in blessing. Sometimes we think we are moving toward a specific plan God has for our lives only to discover God had a greater vision in mind. Abraham climbed the mountain believing he was called to sacrifice his son, Isaac looked for the sheep, but God had neither in mind, He provided a ram and spoke blessing over Abraham and all generations to come.

SPECIAL WORDS

One of the most important elements of the family plan is also a key to strengthening family relationships. That is, speaking words of affirmation and blessing over the individual members of your family. God calls you to this task as the leader of your family. It is an important part of passing forward a lasting legacy.

I can tell you hundreds of stories about the negative effects a lack of spoken blessing creates within families. The results are always the same, but it doesn't have to be this way. God specifically called the leader of the family to bless and be blessed.

I have written at length about the power of *giving* the blessing to your children. But let me share a few thoughts about receiving the blessing as well. In the blessing to Abraham, God essentially said, "And through your offspring, all nations on earth will be blessed, because you have obeyed Me."

Do you really believe that?

For me, that was a tough question because I had doubts of being worthy enough. But as I have grown and matured in my faith, I have come to the place where I can say with confidence, "Yes, I do believe." I am worthy only because I am a child of my Heavenly Father.

Consider ways to speak words of affirmation and blessing over your family. Some families plan special dinners where the family leader will bless each and every person sitting at the table.

Currently, I pray a blessing over our children every night when we tuck them into bed. A blessing, which speaks a bright future, wisdom, friendship, kind heart, good health, loving family, the person they will ultimately marry, is a gift that will help grow your children into whole and healthy adults.

Not only is it important to receive the spoken blessing, we must pass it forward to future generations. It is foundationally rooted—not in emotion or feeling, but in action. Once we implement faith, great things can and will happen for our family. Whatever the form or method, incorporating blessing into the family plan is vital in order to lay the foundation of a bright future for your children.

AFFIRMATION LETTER

It seems in our crazy world we never hear "thank you" and "great job" enough, even from the ones who love us. I find it extremely helpful to affirm children by writing special letters of affirmation telling how proud you are of them.

The letter can include stories or experiences from childhood up to adulthood. I promise you one thing; these letters give so much healing and power to children desperately searching for affirmation from a parent. You can deliver them during your lifetime, have them handed out after your death, or do both.

IN THE FUTURE

As you age and your family orchard grows new trees, technology allows you to encourage future family members even after you have passed away. Letters written with messages to grandchildren or great-grandchildren for special days or with memorable moments in mind can be delivered to them through email or a living relative or the person in charge of your will or trust. It could be they receive an encouraging letter or words of wisdom from a past patriarch/matriarch on that all important sixteenth birthday, their graduation from high school, college, or on their wedding day. This is a great way to have impact well into the future.

LIFE BEGINS AND ENDS WITH RELATIONSHIP

The day you were born, a room full of people celebrated the beginning of your life. In the end, the relationships you nurtured throughout your life are the ones who will usher you from this life into eternal life. Life is about relationships. We are called to live life with an outward focus on others, rather than having an inward focus on ourselves. Speaking words of affirmation and encouragement into others lends strength, value, and worth.

The primary relationships in your life are within your family. How you manage the relationships with those closest to you effects how you manage the relationships of others around you. Just as the trees in an orchard need nourishment and water to grow strong roots and produce healthy fruit, relationships also must be nourished and handled with care.

Abraham understood this too. He nurtured his heart by listening to God's voice; he nurtured his family by speaking God's love into their lives and living out His truth. Abraham nurtured his relationships with others through managing his life well and modeling servant leadership. He also handed out blessings to everyone in his circle of influence and beyond. When you follow his model, you will come under his God-given blessing as well!

RECAP

1. Communication is the key to any long-standing relationship.
2. Blessing and affirming your family should be incorporated into every aspect of family life. No matter how old your children are, or your parents if you are in the sandwich generation, it is *never* too late to bless and affirm them.
3. God created you to have healthy relationships in your life, to encourage your children to learn from you, so they too can nurture healthy relationships in their own lives.

CHAPTER THIRTEEN

MANAGING YOUR STUFF

"In the midst of prosperity, the challenge for believers is to
handle wealth in such a way that it acts as a blessing,
not a curse." —Randy Alcorn

T HE CLOUDS WERE DARK and hung low as I awoke to the sound of
rain hitting the roof of my house. I knew instantly when I looked
out my kitchen window it was going to be a cold, wet winter day in Texas.
I put on my grey sweats, combed my hair, got the paper, woke up the
girls, fed the dogs, and arrived at my kitchen bar to spend a few minutes
catching up on the day's events.

But this day started out a little differently than the others. As soon as
I woke up and hung my legs over the side of the bed, a question popped
into my head. "If I have nothing else in life, is God enough?"

This thought interrupted the usual start of my day. I went on to mull
this question over in my mind throughout the course of the next few days.
I kept thinking about the story of Job, a faithful servant of God who lost
everything, yet never cursed God.

Our world says there is never enough. In fact, success is defined by accumulating the most assets one can in life. We are conditioned from an early age to believe that the more we purchase, the greater our sense of satisfaction in life will grow. Of course, each phase of life is a little different in terms of spending priorities.

The first phase of our adult lives usually begins with pursuing a higher education and determining our career paths. Somewhere included in this phase is marriage, starting a family, and buying a house, but not necessarily in that order. The second phase will most likely have us more established and moving up the ladder in our careers. Then comes maximizing our savings and funding for retirement as our children begin to exit the home to begin their own adult journeys in life. The fourth phase finds us moving into retirement with a desire to experience the freedom we have worked hard to enjoy over most of our lives. In the fifth and final phase of life we begin to reduce the stuff we've accumulated over our lifetime as we desire to return to a more simple and effortless way of living out our final days.

I have come to realize we work a lifetime to earn enough income to acquire, invest in, and amass assets. Then, in our final days, we stress out about how to manage and transfer them to the next generation. Every client I have ever worked with in their advanced years seems overwhelmed as their stuff takes on a life of its own. These individuals find themselves in an unfamiliar place of trying to disperse or transfer their assets while feeling completely overwhelmed.

Is there a better, simpler way? Sure there is, but before we get started down that road, let's deal with the concerns we all encounter as we enter the fifth stage of life.

SURFACE FEARS

The greatest concern I see in the eyes of every elderly person is how they will maintain their independence while making sure they do not outlive their financial resources. The most difficult things to surrender to someone else's control at this stage of life are the management of their money and the ability to transport themselves wherever they chose to go. Yet, these issues must be discussed and a strategy implemented that will provide support during this difficult stage of a person's life.

When parents reach the point when they no longer have the ability to manage their money well and can no longer drive, the time comes for their child or a person they have designated to take over these roles to step in. This is such a difficult place for both parent and child as it escorts in a reversal of roles.

Most families struggle as they enter this phase of life. Parents are fighting to keep their independence and the child does not know when or how to lovingly shift into this phase. The children have trouble as they still see their parents the way they were many years before. They struggle with the reduction of cognitive and physical abilities that come to aging parents. Likewise, parents still visualize their children as teenagers and believe they don't have the ability to perform these necessary duties.

In coaching numerous families I have three simple words I share with them as they enter this phase of life: *honor, respect,* and *acceptance.* There is a proper time to have a family meeting conducted with honor and respect while still protecting the parent's dignity. It is important to discuss with patience and love the options that will allow maximum independence while providing a protective environment.

The acceptance by all parties that this is a phase we will all journey through as we enter the elderly years of life is important. Numerous conversations should occur as several options should be discussed so that all parties feel they have been heard. With increased life expectancy in our country, the need for these family meetings will continue to increase as people are living longer.

How we as parents and children manage these transitional life events are just as important to the family legacy as all of the other steps we have mentioned in establishing a family plan. It is in these challenging times we need to ask for God's wisdom to provide the direction where dignity can be maintained while honor and respect can be preserved.

OUR ASSETS

In the previous chapter I shared my personal journey through infertility. Because of our experience, I understand well how Abraham felt when he called out to God asking, "Who am I going to leave my estate to?" The desire that God placed in all of us, to transfer our blood, sweat, tears, dreams, vision, values, and heart to the next generation, was awakened in our journey as well. I desperately felt the need within my spirit to complete something that could only be achieved by passing forward a baton.

Every family has assets, but they take on different shapes and sizes as each family decides what they value. Some families purchase assets that make them feel good, such as technology items, vehicles, boats, and clothes. Many disciplined families may invest in assets that increase in value such as art, real estate, stocks, bonds, and individual companies. My experience is that all of these items take time, money, and emotional energy to manage in one's life.

The management and transfer of these assets take on importance as they become a component of one's life journey. If handled effectively, they can have maximum impact for future generations. To help achieve this for a family, I have designed a simple four-step process to identify and transfer these assets.

P.A.S.S. is the acronym that will help you effectively transfer assets to the next generation: Preparation, Avoidance, Strategize, and Survey.

PREPARATION

Start with a sheet of paper and begin listing every asset you own: bank accounts, brokerage accounts, life insurance policies, and any other financial institutions. Continue with real estate, personal owned companies, vehicles, motorhomes, boats, etc. Make sure you include cemetery deeds, valuable assets such as heirlooms, gold, silver, and jewelry.

Upon completing the list, define who actually owns every asset. Is it owned by you individually, jointly with a spouse, others, your company, or a trust document? Defining ownership is very important to maximize tax, risk, and estate planning for you and future generations.

The next phase should be an analysis of current income and expenditures. One of the biggest concerns people have is whether or not they will have enough money to last them for their lifetimes. There is a simple way to calculate this. Figure out when you will retire. Calculate the amount of cash you will have at that time by considering inflation and the assumption on current investments. Then, your life expectancy is factored in and we can determine how much you have for retirement, as well as how much you can safely gift, if desired.

In my career, I have noticed that most families will begin some form of gifting as they move into their final phase of their life. I believe this is the beginning of passing the baton for some leaders. The items that are gifted can be of very high financial value or have strong emotional value attached to them. You must determine if the gift will be an irrevocable gift, where the heir can do whatever they want with it when they receive it, or one in which you maintain control of the assets after you have made the gift. You may be scratching your head right about now, saying, "How is it possible to give a gift and still maintain control?"

This is easily accomplished through corporate owned stock or trust documents that allow you to give value away but still control the underlying asset by being an officer or trustee.

It is unacceptable for some parents to see their children mishandle present-day gifts, so maintaining control of how it is used can be important.

Reviewing any existing legal documents is next in line of importance, as I have found once they are signed at the attorney's office, they are placed in a file and rarely reviewed again. If you do not have any documents that will distribute your assets or manage your affairs if you become incapacitated, it is imperative to take care of that now. I have seen a handful of clients resist dealing with "future problems or events" in their lives, but those events can and probably will happen. Being prepared for all situations is as important as becoming effective stewards over the assets we have been given.

AVOIDANCE

Things that are uncomfortable and scary cause us to stick our heads in the sand, hoping that somehow the issue will just go away. We all do it. However, avoidance is the worst thing you can do if you have any intention of leaving a lasting legacy to your heirs.

There are three things that many people have unknowingly put on their avoidance list, and we need to be aware of these important issues that we would prefer to overlook, and face them all head on.

Communication

First and foremost, people avoid clear communication regarding their wishes and desires for the future. Not only that, but I have found very few people who effectively communicate things as simple as the location of legal documents, the list of the family assets, or even how to get into the safe or safety deposit box. In my experience with families who have lost a family leader, more often than not, the heirs are left playing hide-and-seek not only with their assets, but also with locating the legal documents so they can have some form of peace in knowing they are following the wishes and desires of the deceased.

It is your responsibility to put your trust in at least one person with whom you can have in-depth conversations with and document the wishes you want to see carried forward. Consider taping conversations, taking pictures or using videography to record family mementos such as furniture, artwork, and jewelry. If there are special items you want certain children to receive, you need to state your wishes clearly and not leave it for the beneficiaries to fight over.

Family meetings with the next generation are important as you can communicate the business of what will happen if you should die or experience incapacity. The more open communication you can have will ease the pain in the future as the children deal with the loss of your influence and life. Since many families have strained relationships among family members, a third party could be used to facilitate the meeting.

Finances

Many families do not share the specifics about their finances with their adult children or heirs. However, this disclosure is important in protecting the financial well-being of the parent. Do not avoid discussing your family's financial state, and what your vision is for the future of your family. It is important they understand your desires with regard to the management of your finances when you are no longer able to control them yourself.

If you are parents of young children, they need you to teach them financial principles. You may do this by showing them how to manage responsibly the money they have now as well as by modeling Godly financial principles for them to see. They need to see how you invest, how you develop your investor and third-party relationships, and how you want your money used for education, and philanthropic or charitable efforts for future generations.

Health

One of the hardest conversations for children to have with their parents is the discussion of deteriorating health, disability, and incompetence brought on by age. This is especially true if it involves the need to make changes in the person's level of independence and autonomy. Your parents' ability to competently drive and move safely within their home is important for you to monitor. This must be done to physically protect not only the persons themselves while at home and on the road, but also innocent bystanders who may be injured due to the aging person's inability to focus and maintain a certain level of personal safety.

Another issue that hits most everyone as we age is the change in our cognitive abilities regarding the choices being made with how we invest or who we give our money to. I have seen millions of dollars scammed from older parents through phone calls, salesman at the door, and even direct mail requests.

Eventually, the shoe will be on the other foot. We will eventually be the older parent. Having that person you trust and count on is so helpful to provide clarity when you need to make decisions. Independence is important, but having a protective environment that has open communication regarding the issues surrounding your health and finances is also just as important. It is helpful for all of us, regardless of where we fall within the patriarchal line, to acknowledge that these changes will happen, to look for them, and to ask for help when we spot it in someone else or ourselves.

STRATEGIZE

The foundation of every estate plan begins with the legal documents (wills or trusts) that are used to transfer assets to the heirs. Many factors have an effect on these documents, such as: the state of residence, privacy concerns, makeup of the transferred assets, and family harmony. Each and every estate is unique; therefore, I highly suggest finding professionals who will provide you with solid expertise. The cost will be insignificant as it will have maximum impact for future generations.

Your first choice is to have a designated person in place to manage your estate in accordance with your wishes. When referring to a trust, it is the "successor trustee" who manages the details, and when referring to a will it is an "executor" or an "executrix" who manages the details.

They will gather the assets, pay all expenses, and file with probate court if it is a will. Once testamentary letters are received by the judge, they can then sell and transfer the assets to fulfill your wishes.

With a revocable living trust (RLT), if all the assets are in the name of the trust, there will not be a probate filing. For some families, including mine, this becomes a priority to avoid the probate process because of the expense, time delay, and public record of the family's assets. The trustee pays the necessary bills and begins distributions without the time delay.

With either a will or trust, the children can choose to receive the assets outright or be held in a trust. If they are held in a trust, the assets can be protected from creditors and ex-spousal claims. If the estate value is large, you can also add language to the trust that will escape portions of transfer taxes when the children die and will pass tax-free to the grandkids. This is accomplished by utilizing the donor (parents) generation skipping exemption trust (GST).

The utilization of special needs language may be beneficial if included within your document. This language creates provisions for a beneficiary of the estate plan. If they could qualify for various benefits due to disability, the trustee can manage distributions from the trust so the beneficiary can receive the benefits.

There are two types of Powers of Attorney that are needed as part of your estate plan. The first type is a Durable Power of Attorney (DPOA), which allows your spouse or a designated individual to manage your financial affairs if you are incapacitated. These individuals may pay your bills, file taxes, manage investments, and continue current gifting programs.

The second type is a Healthcare Power of Attorney (HPOA), which is beneficial in allowing the same individuals to manage your healthcare needs such as whether to have surgery, facilities to be used, and any future medical decisions that may arise.

If it is your wish, having a living will is helpful as its purpose is to clarify your end of life medical wishes. Should life-support be necessary, the living will specifies your decision with regard to the use of life-support procedures. Providing these instructions to your physician and local hospital eliminates confusion in the future.

So, let's review for a moment. The foundational plans that every family needs are:
- A written plan to transfer your assets (will or trust)
- Financial Power of Attorney
- Healthcare Power of Attorney
- A living will

Other considerations to discuss with your professionals are the benefits of leaving the assets in trust for the children. Also, special needs language, credit shelter protection, and tax planning should be discussed.

Charitable bequest also becomes a viable tool to use in your planning. It can be a present gift or be included in your will or trust to be given to the non-profit organization at your death. Either way it allows you to have a steward's mindset and give back to charities that have had an impact in your family's life.

More advanced strategies such as family partnerships, irrevocable trust, charitable foundations, and gifting programs can provide needed tax relief and generational planning for the family. Researching and discussing these options can help transfer monetary wealth for future generations to use.

Last on this list, but the one that causes the highest level of dislike, are taxes. Can you totally eliminate taxes? Yes, sometimes you can, but if not, at the very least you can minimize the taxes. The three main taxes I help families deal with are income, gift, and estate taxes. Tax planning does change periodically as limits, deductions, and tax rates are changed by our government. The biggest mistake I have seen leaders of the family make is minimizing their tax during their lifetimes but not analyzing how the assets will be taxed in their children's tax bracket or as they transfer to the future generations.

Proper planning is the secret to managing the "avoidance" list as you move forward. Finding a team of professionals that includes a tax professional, attorney, and planner who can help navigate you through this process is important.

SURVEY

This is a final phase of our acronym PASS and I believe it is the most important. You need to periodically survey the plans you have put in place. Have your wishes changed? Are there any additions to the family? Have assets increased or decreased? Do the children have the ability to manage the family company or wealth going forward?

These questions will help you analyze past planning and allow you to make necessary changes. My suggestion is that you review your plans annually and see if they still accomplish your present or future goals. Your legal documents can only be effective as you address side road detours and future expectations.

DO I HAVE ENOUGH?

This question is asked by just about every client with whom I have a conversation. By doing some calculations with conservative assumptions, we can arrive at a number for every individual or family unit regarding the amount of money they need to have in their retirement account to ensure financial security for the rest of their lives.

What is interesting to me is even after there is a plan in place, along with a fully funded retirement account, there still seems to be lingering doubt in most people's minds about having enough money. Why does this kind of self-doubt bubble from within?

I believe it comes down to perspective and faith. If you are truly a person of faith, it is easy to believe God is in control. It takes a separate act of faith to live that out through the daily circumstances of life.

Let's return to the question I began pondering on that rainy winter morning: "If I have nothing else in life, is God enough?" Does my vision for the future of my family and my leadership ability reflect that I believe God is truly all I need? Do my communication efforts, listening skills, and management abilities reflect a belief that I am not an owner of "my stuff" but rather a steward of all that I have accumulated in tangible assets?

So, here is the result of my pondering. If God was enough for Abraham, is He enough for me? The only way I can complete the journey and be the leader my family deserves is to answer with a resounding "yes!" As we act on God's Word and obey His call for our lives, He will bless us and not only provide our tangible needs, such as food, water, and shelter, but also our intangible needs, such as vision, guidance, direction, advice, leadership, communication, relationship, and so much more.

RECAP

1. Locate a professional team that can help you create the plan necessary to implement your legacy, and schedule with them to have that plan periodically evaluated so that it stays up-to-date.
2. Communicate with someone you trust regarding your end-of-life wishes, as well as the location of your necessary documents.
3. Maintain a steward's heart as you manage and then transfer the assets God has specifically provided for your family tree.

CHAPTER FOURTEEN

THE FAMILY LIFE PLAN

"Do not forget the things your eyes have seen or let them
slip from your heart as long as you live. Teach them to your
children and to their children after them."
—Deuteronomy 4:9 NIV

IT WAS A SUNNY AFTERNOON as I closed my door to my truck and slipped my suit jacket over my freshly pressed shirt. I gingerly strolled to the front door of the funeral home and shook hands with the family members I knew. After writing my name in the guestbook, I quickly made my way to the pew.

In my position, working with numerous families, I have grown accustomed to funerals. Today was no different as we came to remember an elderly person that had recently passed away. My experience over the years has taught me there are two types of funerals. The first one involves merely remembering a deceased person's life. The second one is about experiencing a celebration of a life.

This service was of the first type. The person being remembered never really showed any fruits of believing in God or walking with Him on a daily basis. Sure, he had a career, some children, and had accumulated a few assets, but this individual never defined what their living legacy was nor communicated a desire to be remembered as a visionary leader of their family.

How do I know? Because I walked with this family for over ten years and helped them design their estate plan.

Defining a legacy and designing an estate plan are two very different things. An estate plan deals with protecting and transferring the assets. Defining a legacy is about much more. It is applying all five steps that lead to the creation of a family plan; it includes embracing God's call, establishing core values, determining the family vision, building positive relationships, and managing the transfer of assets.

To illustrate this point, I invite you to travel back with me one last time to glean wisdom from the life of Abraham.

ABRAHAM AND THE FIRST FAMILY PLAN

We left Abraham as he was preparing to journey back down the mountain with his son Isaac. He passed the test of faith and God continued to bless not only him but his family orchard. Abraham established the very first generational plan. It is fair to say Abraham is the father of the family life plan!

Looking at the story and life of Abraham, we see he walked out his role as the patriarchal leader of his family and applied the five-step family life plan process.

"Abraham left everything he owned to Isaac" (Genesis 25:5 NIV). First and foremost, Abraham fulfilled God's ultimate call on his life. He was a man of deep faith and was obedient in following God's call. When he and Sarah were faced with infertility, he trusted in God's bigger plan. He took care of his nephew Lot, caring for and mentoring him all along his way. He completed the journey Terah began by leaving Ur and reaching Canaan, the land to which God called him. Abraham said "yes" to God before he knew the magnitude of God's call.

Abraham did not question whether God would come through in the tough circumstances of life; his faith was firm. He believed that God was who He said He was, and He would do what He said He would do. His trust never wavered. Abraham did not tell others how to live; he showed them through his actions. Isn't that what it's really all about? There is a saying I heard once: "People don't respect what you say, until they see they can respect what you live." Abraham understood this. His faith led his actions, his values, his vision, and resulted in God's continued blessing. A blessing handed down infinitely to all future generations.

Second, Abraham was a man who had established values. He knew what was important in life and he stood on those things. Abraham was a man of integrity who walked his talk. He was trustworthy and honest in his dealings with others. He was a good steward of what God had given to him. He was selfless in giving to others.

Abraham was wise in giving advice to his family and those in his circle of influence. He was a good listener. Author John Maxwell says the best leaders are great communicators because they understand the importance of listening to hear another's heart. Abraham not only determined the values that would guide his life, he walked them out so much so that they defined his character and drove the manner in which he valued his relationships. He made sure his family understood the core values they stood upon collectively. These core values are the same values we stand on today as members of the family of faith! They are the core values that define your spiritual family legacy.

Third, Abraham was a man of great vision. Obedience to God's call combined with a God-inspired value system brought forth vision. Abraham was a generational leader; the first generational planner we see recorded in the Bible. Not only did he have vision, but he was also able to communicate this vision to descendants living hundreds of generations later. Even when he could not see the "big picture" clearly, he trusted the end result to God.

A vision alone cannot be successful without action behind it. Abraham lived today with tomorrow in mind. As the leader of his family he understood the importance of managing his relationships well by passing forward faith, value, vision, and blessing. Abraham understood the importance of motivating others to move toward accomplishing their vision through God's power.

Fourth, Abraham was a blessed man of God who blessed others immeasurably. He spoke blessing and words of affirmation and encouragement over those within his family unit as well as in his circle of influence. God enlarged his circle so much that we live within it still today! That's a pretty big circle of influence. He transitioned God's blessing over him onto future generations through the way he managed and genuinely cared for and loved the people around him.

Abraham's son, Isaac, knew his father loved him deeply, and Abraham communicated Isaac's role in carrying forward the family blessing to future generations as well. What a great example for us to follow in our own homes and within the relationships that God has placed us as leaders.

Fifth and last, Abraham was a man of great humility who managed his assets well. What I find interesting about Abraham is that even though by today's standards he might be called uber-wealthy, his material wealth did not define his worth. He was handpicked by God to be the father of many nations and he knew it, yet he chose to walk humbly among men. Abraham understood that money does not define the man, character does. The first four steps culminated into making the fifth step an option and opportunity to influence all future generations immeasurably.

Abraham understood that the richest inheritance he could pass forward to his children, family, circle of influence, and many generations to come was strong faith, values, vision, and blessing, all packaged in the wrappings of humility and well-managed assets. It is this example that defined his character and the reason God chose him to pass forward a spiritual heritage that we as believers have today. Abraham's life continues to impact how we manage our current relationships and establishes the reason why completing a family life plan process is a must and not merely a suggestion.

Abraham left everything he owned to Isaac. Why do you suppose he did this? Because God instructed him that His covenant would only go through Isaac. All the assets were left to Isaac, and they were enormous in value.

Imagine being Ishmael or Isaac and learning under the greatest person of faith. The family life plan was first written and walked out by Abraham, a man who knew God, talked to God, and walked with God.

At the end of this chapter you will begin drafting your own family life plan. In doing so, you will follow Abraham's example. He had the best plan—it was drafted by the Author of Life Himself. The covenant dealt with a call, core values, vision, blessings, and a bright future for Abraham, you, and me. That's right; we have a tree growing in Abraham's orchard because we are part of his family lineage. In fact, with Abraham, we get to study and follow one of the best "celebration of life" examples. He did everything right as he transferred his legacy to the next generation. But there is one more secret we must learn.

IN THE CROSSHAIRS

My favorite time of year is autumn. I love it when the season changes from summer to fall bringing with it lower temperatures and the brilliant colors of the changing leaves. This time of year heightens my senses yet also makes me a little restless. It is the time when the "great provider" part of my testosterone-driven self is drawn to the great outdoors to chase four-legged animals. Pro-animal rights activists need not bother reporting me to some agency. My wife has them all on her speed-dial. As I go out to hunt, she prays for my safety as well as the safety of the animals. It seems to work for the animals more often than not!

Today, let us not explore my hunting ability, but the experience of my hunting buddy, Wayne. I guess we all have big stories to share whether it was a hole-in-one, a huge business deal or the fifteen-pound bass that got away! However, my friend Wayne tells a whopper that makes me shake my head in awe.

One day, Wayne was hunting white tail deer in the hill country of Texas. He was using a normal Texas hunting blind and feeder set-up that many hunters use in our area. As the story goes, the feeder threw some corn on the ground and he began to wait patiently for the big buck.

Much to his surprise a turkey strutted his way to gobble up some corn. The thought of taking home a turkey dinner made his mouth water, yet his goal was bagging a big buck. He succumbed to his desire and shot the turkey at the base of the feeder. Since Wayne had a comfortable seat, he continued to wait for the big buck. A little while later, a raccoon appeared at the feeder. The presence of the turkey startled the raccoon and he ran back into the bush. A few minutes later the raccoon gathered his courage and targeted the turkey for his own dinner. Wayne realized the animal's intention. Since he really wanted that turkey dinner, he eliminated his opponent. The raccoon fell on top of the turkey!

As he giggled about the events that had just transpired, he gave up the hope of anything else coming out of the brush since two shots had now been fired. Still Wayne stayed in the blind for the fun of it. Then just a few minutes later, a doe appeared at the feeder. He looked through his binoculars to see an eight-point buck standing behind her. One last shot and his ultimate goal was achieved—along with the bonus of a raccoon hat and turkey dinner!

Now, I know some people will say this is one tall tale of a hunting story, but I can vouch for my hunting buddy. I have hunted with him for over fifteen years and we are totally different when it comes to our goals. My goal is to have a unique experience and lots of fun. Wayne's goal is all about coming home with meat for the table. Wayne loves to have fun, but the meat is his priority. Neither one of us is wrong, but we see things through a different lens of objectives.

What does Olympic athlete Derek Redmond, Jack the Tailor, Wayne the hunter, and father Abraham have in common? They all lived life with intention. Whatever the goal, they focused on the task at hand by preparing, prioritizing, and focusing on the outcome of their vision!

Great athletes and leaders accomplish greatness in life because they know who they came from, have established their core values, are moving toward their determined vision, strive to build strong family relationships, and manage their assets well. They focus on the result of the process as they walk out their life plans and live legacies that will leave an indelible mark on the lives of future generations. You can begin your family life plan with the same intentionality so you can experience the fruits of your efforts well into the future.

FAMILY LIFE PLAN

Let's begin incorporating the five elements of a family life plan into a brief overview. This is a great way to begin implementing this process into your own family. Once you complete yours, you will have a great guide for informing your family about your generational mindset as well as your plan for how your family will impact other generations down the line. Below is an example of my family plan with nine headings I have used for you to reference as you write your own individual family plan. Underneath each heading, organize your own thoughts into a strong family plan.

Opening Statement

Our family accepts that it is by God's calling that we have been placed in our individual family tree to have impact in this world. We believe that God created us to have fellowship with Him and the only way to do this is through a profession of faith in Jesus, His Son. By teaching the gift of faith, we believe He will provide, protect, and guide our family throughout many generations.

Family Vision

The vision for the family is all members would be well-balanced in every area of their lives. With this balance, they can identify and use the special giftedness they were given by God. Receiving the highest education to fulfill this gift is important as they accept God's call on their lives to have impact wherever He chooses.

Acceptance of the Covenant

We believe that we are a recipient of the Abrahamic Covenant, which entitles us to the same blessings Abraham received; blessings of a bright future, continued legacy, and protection by God.

Family's Core Values

The family's goal is to honor, respect, and encourage each other as we journey through life together. Our family's core values are excellence, faithfulness, generosity, grace, humility, integrity, joy, and love.

Cherished Relationships

The family understands the power of relationships in our lives. The relationships with family friends, mentors and professionals are all unique and we believe that God allows these relationships to be created for encouragement, growth, and fullness. Mentors have been provided in our lives to give wisdom and direction. As a family, we understand the benefit of mentorships and will be encouraged to pass on what we have received to others in our lives.

The following is a list of important relationships for our family:

Friends	Mentors	Professionals
Roy	David	Barry
Larry	Ken	Steve
Wayne	Barry	
Nat	Ron	
Rayleen		
Cindy		

Importance of the Blessing

It is important that the family continues to extend the blessing to each other into the future. The gift of touch, encouragement, affirmation, and being a part of each other's future is important to give and receive.

Financial Principles

The family will transfer the material gifts we have received to the next generation. Our goal as a family is to understand the principal of living through a steward's heart. As we believe God owns all, we will try to manage His assets properly. We will teach all generations the basics of financial management, which include tithing, budgeting, saving, investing, and estate planning.

Philanthropic Mindset

Teaching future generations the benefit of giving is important as they learn a philanthropic mindset. Because of the family's financial blessings, we will teach our children the importance of being a conduit of assets in their lives.

Closing Statement

The family will experience and cherish the laughter, love, and family traditions that are important in our lives. Life is a journey made easier with the people God has placed in our lives. We will encourage all to accept His call as we journey toward a life of significance lived with purpose and passion and having maximum impact on the lives of others.

THE HATCHER FAMILY PLAN

Below is our family plan written out again, except this time, the identifying headings have been removed so you can see what a finished summary would look like.

The Hatcher Family Plan

Our family accepts that it is by God's calling that we have been placed in our individual family tree to have impact in this world. We believe that God created us to have fellowship with him and the only way to do this is through a profession of faith in Jesus, His son. By teaching the gift of faith, we believe He will provide, protect, and guide our family throughout many generations.

The vision for our family is all members will be well-balanced in every area of their lives. With this balance, they can identify and use the special giftedness they were given by God. Receiving the highest education to fulfill this gift is important as they accept God's call on their lives to have impact wherever he chooses.

We believe that we are recipients of the Abrahamic Covenant which entitles us to the same blessings Abraham received; blessings of a bright future, continued legacy and protection by God.

Our family's goal is to honor, respect, and encourage each other as we journey through life together. Our family's Core Values are excellence, faithfulness, generosity, grace, humility, integrity, joy, and love.

Our family understands the power of relationships in our lives. Family friends, professional and mentor relationships are all unique and we believe that God allows these relationships to be created for encouragement, growth and fullness. Mentors have been provided in our life to give wisdom and direction. As a family, we understand the benefit of mentorships and will be encouraged to pass on what we have received to others in our life.

The following is a list of important relationships for our family:

Friends	*Mentors*	*Professionals*
Roy	David	Barry
Larry	Ken	Steve
Wayne	Barry	
Nat	Ron	
Rayleen		
Cindy		

It is important that our family extends the blessing to each other in the future. The gift of touch, encouragement, affirmation, and being a part of each other's future is important to give and receive.

We will transfer the material gifts we have received to the next generation. Our goal as a family is to understand the principal of living through a steward's heart. As we believe God owns all, we will try to manage His assets properly. We will teach the basics of financial management to all generations which include tithing, budgeting, retirement, investment management, and estate planning.

Teaching future generations the benefit of giving is important as they learn a philanthropic mindset. Because of our financial blessings, we will teach our children the importance of being a conduit of assets in their life.

We will experience and cherish the laughter, love, and family traditions that are important in our lives. Life is a journey made easier with the people God has placed in our life. We will encourage all to accept his call as we journey toward a life of significance lived with purpose, passion, and to have maximum impact on the lives of others.

Use the nine headings, begin creating a family plan. If you desire, add action points and explicit instructions to each of the nine. The ultimate goal is the family plan will be the foundation that your family will use to measure opportunities and choices to make.

It can and should be reviewed and updated on a regular basis. Your life experiences, relationships, and growth will give you new desires and ideas as you choose what is important for you and future generations. Since that is now complete, let's move to one last strategy.

PASS THE BATON

When I ran track in school, I was always amazed at the fluidness of our 440-yard relay team. Every teammate would sprint for 110 yards and hand the baton to the next sprinter. There was a transfer lane where the baton had to be passed to the other runner or the team would be eliminated.

The timing was duplicated multiple times in our practice to achieve efficiency. Tape marks were applied to the track to let you know the split second to accelerate so the incoming runner and outgoing runner would be at the same speed when the exchange occurred.

The incoming runner would call out, "Stick!" while extending his left hand with the baton. The next runner would extend his right hand, grab the baton, and explode toward the next runner.

As I watch the 400-meter relay in the Olympics, it is the same fluidness that always mesmerizes me when the relay team completes their task. Their goal is to win the race with efficiencies that have been honed through multiple hours of training. The giftedness of each runner is easy to see, but the real beauty is in the effectiveness of the team.

Is your family legacy any different? No! Are you not running a race of stewardship ready to pass the baton to the next generation?

As I have studied the life of Abraham, my conclusion is—yes.

Just as God called Abraham to go, leave, and follow, He gave Abraham and all of us one more command. "Stick!" Pass the baton.

RECAP

1.   Become intentional as you focus on your family plan and the impact it will have for future generations.
2.   Cast a bold vision for your family tree and the impact it can have within your family.
3.   Prepare to efficiently transfer "the baton" to the next generation.

A Closing Word

• • • • •

THE ABRAHAM-CENTERED JOURNEY we just completed has shown us that we all receive a call, vision, blessings, and bright future for our family tree just as Abraham did. It is our choice to harness these truths to define the impact we are called to provide for future generations.

Our world is moving at such a great speed that the answer to the question, "Why am I here?" is hard to comprehend.

The journey I personally have been traveling has assured me that I can answer that question ... by defining my legacy for my family tree.

My hope is this will have impact in your life and your children's lives. As you receive what is truly given to believers of Christ, our decisions are important as we choose to leave a lasting legacy, as Abraham did, or live like Lot—with no positive impact at all, except to maybe be a model of "what NOT to do."

It was laid on my heart to write this book to emphasize "why" long-term legacy planning is so important, and in doing so, I was able to give some basic guidelines to help you in that process. Because every family is unique in its vision, your needs will also be unique. I encourage you to find advisors and professionals in your area that can assist you with this ever-important process of ensuring your legacy lives on. Please feel free to contact us at any time or visit our website at guyhatcher.com for more planning tips, worksheets, and resources to help build your plan.

May your family orchard be beautiful, full of fruit, and deeply rooted for eternity. That is so very possible because our source of water, light, and love is the same Creator.

CPSIA information can be obtained at www.ICGtesting.com
Printed in the USA
LVOW06s0413201113

361982LV00002B/3/P